SpringerBriefs in Economics

SpringerBriefs present concise summaries of cutting-edge research and practical applications across a wide spectrum of fields. Featuring compact volumes of 50 to 125 pages, the series covers a range of content from professional to academic. Typical topics might include:

- A timely report of state-of-the art analytical techniques
- A bridge between new research results, as published in journal articles, and a contextual literature review
- A snapshot of a hot or emerging topic
- An in-depth case study or clinical example
- A presentation of core concepts that students must understand in order to make independent contributions

SpringerBriefs in Economics showcase emerging theory, empirical research, and practical application in microeconomics, macroeconomics, economic policy, public finance, econometrics, regional science, and related fields, from a global author community.

Briefs are characterized by fast, global electronic dissemination, standard publishing contracts, standardized manuscript preparation and formatting guidelines, and expedited production schedules.

More information about this series at http://www.springer.com/series/8876

Blanca de-Miguel-Molina ·
Virginia Santamarina-Campos ·
María de-Miguel-Molina · Rafael Boix-Doménech
Editors

Music as Intangible Cultural Heritage

Economic, Cultural and Social Identity

Editors
Blanca de-Miguel-Molina
Universitat Politècnica de València
Valencia, Spain

Virginia Santamarina-Campos
Universitat Politècnica de València
Valencia, Spain

María de-Miguel-Molina
Universitat Politècnica de València
Valencia, Spain

Rafael Boix-Doménech
Universitat de València
Valencia, Spain

ISSN 2191-5504   ISSN 2191-5512 (electronic)
SpringerBriefs in Economics
ISBN 978-3-030-76881-2   ISBN 978-3-030-76882-9 (eBook)
https://doi.org/10.1007/978-3-030-76882-9

© The Editor(s) (if applicable) and The Author(s) 2021. This book is an open access publication.
Open Access This book is licensed under the terms of the Creative Commons Attribution 4.0 International License (http://creativecommons.org/licenses/by/4.0/), which permits use, sharing, adaptation, distribution and reproduction in any medium or format, as long as you give appropriate credit to the original author(s) and the source, provide a link to the Creative Commons license and indicate if changes were made.

The images or other third party material in this book are included in the book's Creative Commons license, unless indicated otherwise in a credit line to the material. If material is not included in the book's Creative Commons license and your intended use is not permitted by statutory regulation or exceeds the permitted use, you will need to obtain permission directly from the copyright holder.

The use of general descriptive names, registered names, trademarks, service marks, etc. in this publication does not imply, even in the absence of a specific statement, that such names are exempt from the relevant protective laws and regulations and therefore free for general use.

The publisher, the authors and the editors are safe to assume that the advice and information in this book are believed to be true and accurate at the date of publication. Neither the publisher nor the authors or the editors give a warranty, expressed or implied, with respect to the material contained herein or for any errors or omissions that may have been made. The publisher remains neutral with regard to jurisdictional claims in published maps and institutional affiliations.

This Springer imprint is published by the registered company Springer Nature Switzerland AG
The registered company address is: Gewerbestrasse 11, 6330 Cham, Switzerland

Foreword: Music as Intangible Heritage in Memories from the Past and Visions for the Future

Spain is one of the countries where I conducted my studies on cultural and creative industries and I have many memories that tie me to this country. I remember the first time I went to Valencia. I was studying the processes of cultural districtualisation in cities of art. The first things that caught my eye, walking along the Paseo de la Alameda, where the Turia river flowed in the past, were the Palau de la Música auditorium and, at its end, the Ciudad de las Artes y las Ciencias designed by the Valencian architect Santiago Calatrava and Felix Candela with the splendid Oceanogràfic aquarium and the Palau de les Arts opera house (Boix et al., 2017). These symbolic representations of music and science as material heritage, together with theatres and museums, remain indelibly etched in my memory. In subsequent years, I continued to gain a better understanding of cultural and creative industry maps in Spain by studying important creative and culturaFl clusters (Lazzeretti et al., 2008; Lazzeretti, 2011; Boix & Lazzeretti, 2012; Lazzeretti & Parrilli, 2012).

Valencia as a city of culture is now also perceived as a creative metropolis capable of combining tradition and new technologies, a space where many of the local development principles suggested by one of the greatest Italian economists of the twentieth century, Giacomo Becattini (2004), can be successfully implemented.

These are important places, not only from an economic point of view, but also from a natural, historical and artistic standpoint, where the so-called "awareness of places" is born in the communities of people and businesses that live there in harmony, creating traditions, culture and development.

> [..] and in the beginning, there was the consciousness of place. We start from the village community and going back through history we meet the polis and the free Commune. [..] The civil economy was born here and then loses the north wind. My idea is that it remains strong until the beginning of the Renaissance. Then with the power that moves from nobility to the industrial bourgeoisie and first becomes professional consciousness and then with the mechanization induced by the industrial revolution and with Fordist capitalism, class consciousness. (Becattini, 2015: 156; 159)

In the past, we defined these locations as being places of 'high culture' and we identified them thanks to their symbolic capital represented by the set of material and immaterial, cultural, artistic, natural and human resources that represent them.

Cultural, Artistic and Natural Heritage (CANH) must be thought of as the discriminating factor for marking the city of art out from the 'non-artistic' one, [..] CANH should signify a set of material and immaterial resources that can be traced back to its three main components - artistic, cultural and environmental (Lazzeretti, 1997: 669) i.e., the distinctive traits of an HC Place. Among the first, we can obviously number the set of artistic assets and art structures; the second designates the set of activities, behaviours, habits and customs that makes a specific place different from any other; the third component comprises specific elements of urban, naturalistic and environmental landscapes. This 'objective' notion of CANH can certainly measure the 'real artistic potential of a place', but it cannot determine in an exhaustive manner its overall value. A second element, a subjective one, should be taken into account; that is, the worth of CANH as 'symbolic capital', i.e. the value of the city perceived in the collective imaginary of its various audiences. (Lazzeretti, 2003: 639)

More recent research also adds to these factors the 'awareness of place', an intangible and idiosyncratic capital that we can define as a set of values and beliefs that contribute to qualifying High Culture places, distinguishing them from those that are not. They preserve the 'soul' of places, becoming 'anchors and antidotes' to tackle the risks of the dark side of the new algorithmic society, characterised by the dualism of 'online and on life' of citizens and consumers. In this period, intangible capital becomes more relevant than material capital (Vecco, 2010), made more adaptable and malleable by new ICT technologies, while artistic, natural cultural heritages are fully involved and sometimes transformed.

In the age of social networks marked by the end of the theories where everyone has access to communications and is looking for visibility to have 'recognition', cultural factors and territories are anchors and antidotes to recognize between reality and fiction. (Lazzeretti, 2020:16)

One of the most representative events that make up the intangible and idiosyncratic resources of the city of Valencia is the traditional festivity of *Las Fallas* recognised by the UNESCO as an example of the Intangible Cultural Heritage of Humanity in 2016. It is a complex, participatory event of national and international significance where a multiplicity of cultural resources are involved: from music, to dance, to circus activities, all embedded in the Valencian Region. These resources are exploited economically and socially but, above all, must be protected and preserved for the value of their authenticity. The *Las Fallas* festivity is one of the most famous cases of the so-called *economía de la fiestas* which represents a founding element of identity in Spanish society as a whole (Ruiz Feo, 2020; Rius-Ulldemolins et al., 2020).[1] The economic impact of *fiestas* has been widely discussed in the literature. Some studies have centred on the *Semana Santa* and the Seville Fair (Palma Martos et al., 2014), others have studied flamenco in its three components of singing, dancing, and guitar, which is also included in the UNESCO list of Intangible Cultural Heritage of Humanity (Heredia-Carroza et al., 2020; Palma Martos et al., 2017); and the festival of *Sanfermines* with the bull-running in Pamplona, narrated by Ernest Hemingway

---

[1] The *Fallas* Festival is a cultural activity which takes place annually. It is held in streets, squares and districts, and became the city's main festivity in 1936. Its ritual work extends to nearly a hundred more locations, without paradoxically losing its original essence. The event was included in the list of Intangible Cultural Heritage of Humanity in 2016, and has strong roots in Valencian society.

in the famous book *Fiesta* (Muñoz Molina, 2005; Ravenscroft & Matteucci, 2003). These are interesting examples of the applications of economic enhancement theories to further culture and local development.

If we consider the regions of Spain and, in particular, the Valencian Region, we find another important intangible cultural resource which is widespread throughout the territory: music, considered by many to be 'a resource of the community.' In this sense, music comprehends various genres, institutional varieties and professionalisms. It goes from the music of the theatres and concert halls to the ethnic, popular music of the *bandas de musica* that animate the regions, reaching even the smallest peripheral areas (Rausell and Montagut, 2016; Montagut and Rausell, 2018). It is a resource with a strong capacity for social aggregation that goes beyond the boundaries of traditional music education by generating a local identity and carrying out a social function. The multiple forms of aggregation that music feeds can be considered an example of what the district theory defines as "social capital" (Putnam, 1993) and we find it in many Spanish regions, such as the cultural and religious organisations of the Andalusian *hermandades*, cornerstones of the organisation of the *Semana Santa* festivities.

The symbolic and identity value of music has always accompanied major social transformations. This is the case of the ballads of Joan Baez, such as "We shall overcome", and Bob Dylan, with "Blowing in the wind", which accompanied the political and youth movements of the 60s and 70s, as well as the songs of Francesco Guccini, such as "La Locomotiva", in the years of student protests in Italy. However, music is also poetry linked to the territories and their identity. This is testified by composers such as Fabrizio De Andrè with his Liguria or Joaquín Sabina with Andalusia, but also by orchestras that reproduce popular music, such as the maestro Roberto De Simone and the Nuova Compagnia di Canto Popolare of Naples. They have all contributed to bringing the focus back from the economy to society and, in particular, to the societal function of culture:

> A new phase characterized by a 'social enhancement of culture' has begun to assert itself, revealing – also thanks to the current economic crisis– a societal function of cultural heritage where the primacy of social aspects over economic aspects in cultural policies is explicitly being acknowledged. Arts and culture have the power to connect people and become a strategic tool for the safeguarding of the identity and authenticity of places and local communities facing the rise of the excesses of the entertainment society. Additionally, the countervailing factors of social exclusion, the generation of new clusters of high-value productive activities and jobs, and the pursuit of an inclusive urban society are important objectives to which art and culture can significantly contribute. (Lazzeretti, 2012: 230)

Nowadays, the scenario has changed. We have moved from economic and social enhancement to the technological enhancement of culture. The focus has shifted from the real/material dimension to the virtual/immaterial one. Thus, the values connected with physical proximity, useful for the diffusion of the Marshallian creative atmosphere discussed by the Marshallian industrial districts' theory, have sometimes been replaced by the value of the immaterial, of cognitive proximity, which is easier to combine with liquid, global and transversal capitalism defined by the economy of relationships, of technologies and cities. A new kind of geography has been designed where coordinates of 'space and time' have progressively faded, borders have become nuanced and the economy of complexity has generated a new idea of immaterial, "documedial capitalism" (Ferraris, 2017) where information and documents are goods exchanged on the web, adding another dimension to online life: online life in the *isosphere* (Floridi, 2014).

The technological enhancement of culture faces new risks and opportunities. Some of these are related to the development of new cultural and creative industries such as videogames, the rise of digital humanities and the risks of memory loss, alienation and the loss of fundamental rights of individuals:

> In the era of the anthropology of machines and the ecology of humans, it is necessary to reset everything and go back to the beginning, to the natural world and the availability of resources. There are therefore three categories we have to create value, culture and development: Natural Resources, Human Resources and also Machines. In this way we will be able to imagine new models of sustainable culture-driven development aimed at the preservation, conservation and technological enhancement of Diversity, be it Natural, Human, Artistic, Cultural and Digital, where the latter represents the synthesis of the interaction between humans and machines. (Lazzeretti, 2020: 6)

This book extends the discussion about the value of music in this new phase of the relationship between economy, culture, society and technology. Music is the intangible cultural resource that has anticipated this transformation more than others. The Muse Terpsichore represents a resource and a universal language that perhaps can become a bridge between the natural language of artists and the artificial one of machines, or a border area for hybridisation and creativity. The history of music teaches us this. It has always mashed up contaminations and re-combinations between word and sound—be they human invention, taken from nature or created by technologies—or mixing different musical genres.

If we try to briefly retrace the main technological innovations that have influenced the diffusion/production of music since the end of the 19th century, Thomas Edison's phonograph and Emile Berliner's gramophone spring to mind (Hanson, 2016). Music has marked many great transformations not only in products but also in consumer behaviour and styles. We remember the 'vinyl revolution' in the 30s that accompanied the great crisis of 1929. This was followed by the jukeboxes of the legendary 50s, music tapes in the 60s, compact discs in the 80s, and then the Mp3 later on. These years have moved toward the transition from the analogical to the digital paradigm. The music sector has brought a series of destructive technological innovations, anticipating what happened subsequently with other forms of art. In the present, the emergence and diffusion of the Internet and social networks have amplified and multiplied the effects of digital transformation thanks to the spread of the sharing and experience economy. Streaming music and music platforms are emerging together with new professions that have radically changed not only the production models of record companies but, above all, consumption models (Eriksson et al., 2019).

Artists have recombined musical productions, and companies have redesigned new creative, symbolic and industrial spaces (Innocenti & Lazzeretti, 2019; Klement & Strambach, 2019) through massive use of technology, not only to disseminate music but also to compose it, as demonstrated by the frequent cases of compositions made by artificial intelligence. An example is MuseNet,[2] a deep neural network that can generate musical compositions with 10 different instruments and can combine genres from country music to Mozart or the Beatles. Another example is the AIVA (Artificial Intelligence Visual Artist) program.[3] Thus, the dark side of technology has emerged with its negative effects on the protection of copyright, on consumer profiling, on the growing spread of the phenomenon of piracy, making the music sector an important case of a shadow economy (Wajsman et al., 2016). This has led to rethinking the importance of copyright and how difficult it is to protect with the old rules which were established before the new digital revolution.

Music as intangible heritage, therefore, drives us in the different social, cultural and economic transformations of our century. In the past, it was enough to evoke Australian Aboriginal "Songlines," as told by Bruce Chatwin, to explain that music is also geography. However, new protagonists are emerging in the era of the anthropology of machines and the ecology of humans (Harari, 2016). We will have to interact with them not only on an economic and social level but, above all, on a cultural level.

This book is about all this and much more. The topics covered link music to emergent themes such as cultural and creative industries, social capital, gender, social innovation, the global value chain and business models, between tradition and new modernity. It is therefore with great pleasure that I invite you to read this volume published by my Spanish colleagues which is not only a collection of contributions on the economic enhancement of culture but also a "musical" vision of a whole community.

Luciana Lazzeretti
University of Florence, Florence, Italy

Acknowledgments This book has been written as part of the agreement "*Análisis identitario, político y económico del Paisaje Cultural Inmaterial de la de la Banda Primitiva de Llíria*" (Identity, political and economic analysis of the Intangible Cultural Landscape of the Banda Primitiva de Llíria), coordinated by V. Santamarina Campos and with the participation of M.A. Carabal Montagud, B. de Miguel Molina and M. de Miguel Molina.

References

Becattini, G. (2004). *Industrial districts: A new approach to industrial change*. Edward Elgar Publishing.
Becattini, G. (2015). *La coscienza dei luoghi: il territorio come soggetto corale*. Donzelli editore.

---

[2] https://openai.com/blog/musenet.

[3] https://www.aiva.ai/about.

Boix, R., Rausell, P., & Abeledo, R. (2017). The Calatrava model: reflections on resilience and urban plasticity. *European Planning Studies, 25*(1), 29–47.

Boix-Domenech, R., & Lazzeretti, L. (2012). Las industrias creativas en España: una panorámica. Investigaciones Regionales. *Journal of Regional Research, 22,* 181–206.

Eriksson, M., Fleischer, R., Johansson, A., Snickars, P., & Vonderau, P. (2019). *Spotify teardown: Inside the black box of streaming music.* Mit Press.

Ferraris, M. (2017). *Postverità e altri enigmi.* Bologna: Il Mulino.

Floridi, L. (2014). *The fourth revolution: How the infosphere is reshaping human reality.* Oxford: OUP.

Hanson, R. E. (2016). *Mass communication: Living in a media world.* Sage Publications.

Harari, Y. N. (2016). *Homo Deus: A brief history of tomorrow.* Random House.

Heredia-Carroza, J., Palma Martos, L., & Aguado, L. F. (2020). How to Measure Intangible Cultural Heritage Value? The Case of Flamenco in Spain. *Empirical Studies of the Arts,* 1-22.

Innocenti, N., & Lazzeretti, L. (2019). Do the creative industries support growth and innovation in the wider economy? Industry relatedness and employment growth in Italy. *Industry and Innovation, 26*(10), 1152–1173.

Klement, B., & Strambach, S. (2019). Innovation in creative industries: Does (related) variety matter for the creativity of urban music scenes? *Economic Geography, 95*(4), 385–417.

Lazzeretti, L. (2003). City of art as a high culture local system and cultural districtualization processes: The cluster of art restoration in Florence. *International Journal of Urban and Regional Research, 27*(3), 635–648.

Lazzeretti, L. (2011). Culture as a source for growth and change: some evidence from cultural clusters in Andalusia. In B. Asheim, R. Boschma, P. Cooke, R. Martín, D. Schwartz, & F. Todtling (Eds.), *Handbook of regional innovation and growth* (pp. 350–362). Cheltenham: Edward Elgar.

Lazzeretti, L. (2012). The resurge of the "societal function of cultural heritage". An introduction. *City, Culture and Society, 4*(3), 229–233.

Lazzeretti, L. (2020). What is the role of culture facing the digital revolution challenge? Some reflections for a research agenda. *European Planning Studies,* 1–21.

Lazzeretti, L., Boix, R., & Capone, F. (2008). Do creative industries cluster? Mapping creative local production systems in Italy and Spain. *Industry and innovation, 15*(5), 549–567.

Lazzeretti, L., & Parrilli, M. D. (2012). New focus of economic reactivation in Spain: creative industries in the Basque Country. In Innovation, global change and territorial resilience. Edward Elgar Publishing.

Molina, Y. M. (2005). Las corridas de toros en San Fermín: El riesgo, la muchedumbre y el hedonismo. *AD-minister, 6,* 28–48.

Montagut, J., & Rausell, P. (2018). Impacto económico y social de las sociedades musicales en la Meseta de Requena-Utiel. *Oleana, 32,* 293–310.

Palma Martos, L., Palma Martos, M. L., Rodríguez, A., Martín, J. L., & Cascajo, I. (2017). Live Flamenco in Spain: A dynamic analysis of supply with managerial implications. *International Journal of Arts Management,* 58-70.

Palma Martos, L., Palma Martos, M. L., & Martin Navarro, J. L. (2014). La integración entre cultura y economía. El caso de las Fiestas de Primavera de Sevilla. *Estudios de Economía Aplicada, 32,* 287–308.

Palma Martos, M. L., Palma Martos, L., & Aguado, L. F. (2013). Determinants of cultural and popular celebration attendance: the case study of Seville Spring Fiestas. *Journal of Cultural Economics, 37*(1), 87–107.

Putnam, R. (1993). The prosperous community: Social capital and public life. *The american prospect, 13*(Spring), Vol. 4.

Rausell, P., & Montagut, J. (2016). El Valor del patrimonio musical valenciano. Una aproximación desde la economía de la cultura. Marzal, R. (ed.) *El valor cultural de la música. Punto de partida para el estudio del patrimonio musical* (pp. 183–192). Thomson Reuters.

Ravenscroft, N., & Matteucci, Z. (2003). The Festival as Carnivalesque: Social Governance and Control at Pamplona's San Fermin Fiesta. *Tourism, Culture and Communication, 4*(1), 1–15.

Rius-Ulldemolins, J., Gisbert, V., & Vera, C. (2020). Traditional festivities, political domination and social reproduction: Case analysis of Valencia's Fallas. *European Journal of Cultural and Political Sociology,* 1–28.

Ruiz, F. (2020). Tourism marketing and local celebrations: A case study in Valencia's Fallas. *Cuadernos de Turismo, 45,* 363–587.

Vecco, M. (2010). A definition of cultural heritage: From the tangible to the intangible. *Journal of cultural heritage, 11*(3), 321–324.

Wajsman, N., Arias Burgos, C., Davies, C. (2016). *The economic cost of Ipr infringement in the recorded music industry.* EUIPO.

Contents

Economic, Cultural and Social Identity

Introduction: Music, from Intangible Cultural Heritage to the Music Industry 3
Blanca de-Miguel-Molina and Rafael Boix-Doménech

The Impact of the Music Industry in Europe and the Business Models Involved in Its Value Chain 9
Blanca de-Miguel-Molina, Rafael Boix-Doménech, and Pau Rausell-Köster

The Role of Public Policies in Enhancing Cultural and Creative Industries: An Analysis of Public Policies Related to Music in Colombia 27
Flor Marleny Gómez-Reyes, Daniel Catalá-Pérez, and María de-Miguel-Molina

Soundcool: A Business Model for Cultural Industries Born Out of a Research Project 41
Nuria Lloret-Romero, Jorge Sastre-Martínez, Crismary Ospina-Gallego, and Stefano Scarani

Breaking the Gender Gap in Rap/Hip-Hop Consumption 51
María Luisa Palma-Martos, Manuel Cuadrado-García, and Juan D. Montoro-Pons

Music and Territory: The Case of Bands in the Valencian Region

The Intangible Cultural Landscape of the Banda Primitiva de Llíria ... 69
Virginia Santamarina-Campos, José Luis Gasent-Blesa, Pau Alcocer-Torres, and Mª Ángeles Carabal-Montagud

Music for the Moors and Christians Festivities as Intangible Cultural Heritage: A Specific Genre for Wind Bands in Certain Spanish Regions 101
Daniel Catalá-Pérez and Gabino Ponce-Herrero

The Impact of the COVID-19 Pandemic on Musical Societies in the Valencian Region, Spain 119
María Ángeles Carabal-Montagud, Guillem Escorihuela-Carbonell, Virginia Santamarina-Campos, and Javier Pérez-Catalá

Conclusions: Music as an Economic, Social, Cultural, Creative and Resilient Activity 139
María de-Miguel-Molina and Virginia Santamarina-Campos

Abbreviations

B.C.	Before Christ
BOE	Boletín Oficial del Estado (Official State Gazette)
CANH	Cultural, Artistic and Natural Heritage
CCIs	Cultural and Creative Industries
DIY	Do-it-yourself
FSMCV	Federación de Sociedades Musicales de la Comunitat Valenciana (Valencian Region Federation of Musical Societies)
GDP	Gross Domestic Product
ICT	Information and Communication Technologies
IFPI	International Federation of the Phonographic Industry
IMPF	Independent Music Publishers International
INE	Instituto Nacional de Estadística (National Statistics Institute)
IVAM	Instituto Valenciano de Arte Modern (Valencian Modern Art Museum)
IVC	Institut Valencià de Cultura (Valencian Institute of Culture)
MS	Musical societies
RTVE	Corporación de Radio y Televisión Española (Spanish Radio and Television Corporation)
SGAE	Sociedad General de Autores y Editores (General Society of Authors and Publishers)
SMEs	Small and Medium Enterprises
TVE	Televisión Española (Spain's public television company)
UDP	Unión Democrática de Pensionistas (Democratic Pensioners Union)
UNCTAD	United Nations Conference on Trade and Development
UNESCO	United Nations Educational, Scientific and Cultural Organization
WASBE	World Association for Symphonic Bands and Ensembles

Economic, Cultural and Social Identity

Introduction: Music, from Intangible Cultural Heritage to the Music Industry

Blanca de-Miguel-Molina and Rafael Boix-Doménech

Our first contact with music is almost certainly in our childhood when our parents sing lullabies to us at bedtime. In a community where music is important, these songs are likely to be successfully transmitted from one generation to the next. This is similar to the concept of intangible cultural heritage and how it is transmitted. Intangible cultural heritage, according to the UNESCO's 2003 Convention (2018a), refers to "the oral traditions and expressions, performing arts, social practices, rituals and festive events" that are transmitted from generation to generation. The UNESCO List of Intangible Cultural Heritage has been extended with new inscriptions since 2008. The terms music and song are present in 304 of the 584 elements on the list (52%), referring to music alone or combined with other dimensions such as dance and poetry. Table 1 shows some famous examples that feature on the list, such as the Tango in Argentina and Uruguay, Spanish flamenco, the fado from Portugal and Jamaican reggae music (2018).

Why have these elements been considered expressions of intangible cultural heritage and added to the list by the UNESCO? The answer is related to artistic expressions which are important factors of identity for communities in specific territories. For example, the Tango nomination stated that it is part of the cultural identity of inhabitants in the La Plata region, while flamenco is synonymous with identity in the Spanish regions of Andalusia, Murcia and Extremadura. Although convention points out that communities are more open than territories, as generations move to other countries or to cities, intangible heritage must be present in the territory. Communities in the cases cited recognise these expressions as heritage and work

---

B. de-Miguel-Molina (✉)
Department of Business Organisation, Universitat Politècnica de València, Valencia, Spain
e-mail: bdemigu@omp.upv.es

R. Boix-Doménech
Departament d'Estructura Econòmica, Universitat de València, Valencia, Spain
e-mail: rafael.boix@uv.es

© The Author(s) 2021
B. de-Miguel-Molina et al. (eds.), *Music as Intangible Cultural Heritage*, SpringerBriefs in Economics,
https://doi.org/10.1007/978-3-030-76882-9_1

Table 1 Examples of musical heritage on the UNESCO list

Intangible cultural heritage	Year in the list	Country	Territory	Concept	SDG
Music and dance of Dominican Bachata	2019	Dominican Republic		Music, dance, social gathering	
Reggae music	2018	Jamaica		Music	10
Music and dance of the merengue	2016	Dominican Republic		Music and dance	10
Traditional Vallenato music*	2015	Colombia	Greater Magdalena region	Music	
Fado	2011	Portugal	Lisbon	Music and poetry	
Mariachi	2011	Mexico		Music and orchestras	
Flamenco	2010	Spain	Andalusia, Murcia, Extremadura	Music, dance, instruments	
Tango	2009	Argentina and Uruguay	Buenos Aires and Montevideo	Music and dance	16

*On the List in Need of Urgent Safeguarding
Source https://ich.unesco.org/en/lists

together with national and local authorities to ensure this intangible heritage is safeguarded and transmitted from one generation to the next through education and festivals (UNESCO, 2009, 2010, 2011a, 2018b). Therefore, communities create, maintain and transmit intangible heritage (UNESCO, 2011b). The UNESCO also verifies that the community's participation in the nomination process is carried out following the Free, Prior and Informed Consent (FPIC) approach. This is a tool that the United Nations requires in projects to ensure the participation of involved communities (FAO, 2016).

The UNESCO indicates the importance of safeguarding. From a cultural perspective, carrying out an inventory of cultural heritage and making it available to people contributes to the safeguarding process. Digitalisation has enabled the inventory of sound archives that can be conserved and transmitted to future generations (Gonzaga Videira & Martins Rosa, 2017). The existence of museums related to the musical expressions listed as intangible heritage is an important factor in collecting and preserving traditions in audiovisual archives (Stoffel & Victor, 2017). The four examples of intangible heritage cited have museums associated with their musical styles which ensure their transmission to the community, younger generations and tourists.

The preservation of musical heritage requires the transmission of expressions from one generation to the next. From a business point of view, record labels and other firms in the music industry value chain can support music heritage inventory and safeguarding. In some of the examples cited, the nomination indicates that the cultural expressions included in the list have influenced other musical styles. This is especially true when singers and bands become famous and make a style known across the world. It is more likely that their music will be recorded and safeguarded for future generations. For example, the catalogue of Universal Music Group includes recordings by Bob Marley. However, labels are businesses, and they need to ensure the sustainability of their own firms. Cooperation with the UNESCO might help to increase the number of styles available in their catalogues, especially those in need of safeguarding.

Transmission of music genres, as in the cases of fado and reggae, increases because people listen to music and select these styles, because recorded labels include these styles in their catalogues and they are then distributed through streaming platforms, and because experiences are designed with a focus on music, with local culture being integrated into these experiences. These experiences include festivals, live music performances and experiences designed by local guests for tourists.

The music industry covers more than intangible cultural heritage. The number of people who listen to music everyday indicates the importance of music in our lives. If the percentage of people listening to music is high, the styles of music they can discover every day will increase (Fitterman Radbill, 2017). In Spain, 70.6% of people and 90% of students listen to music every day.[1] Moreover, the devices most used for listening to music are the radio (65.7%) and mobile phones (48.5%), while 53.2% connect directly to the Internet. Data indicate that 22.3% of people in Spain listen to recorded flamenco music and 10.7% listen to reggae music. In Colombia, the most popular music genre in recorded music in 2017 was Vallenato.[2] This genre has been on the UNESCO List as Cultural Heritage in Need of Urgent Safeguarding since 2015. In Argentina, the Tango is not among the most listened to genres, ranking tenth in importance and listened to by 34.5% of the population,[3] while rock is listened to by 68% and reggaeton by 54.2%. All these data indicate the influence of music in other territories.

Music is distributed through music streaming platforms, radio, television and also via podcasts. In 2019, 21.4% of people in Spain had a subscription to a music streaming platform, 10% of whom had a premium subscription. Around 20% of people with a subscription listened to flamenco and 16% to reggae music through their streaming service. IFPI (2019) estimated that 89% of people across the world listen to music through streaming platforms. However, this percentage is lower when age is considered and drops to 54% for people between 35 and 64 years old. The number of platforms available on the market has increased in recent years, offering the different styles available to a wider audience. They feature those cited in Table 1 in

---

[1] Ministry of Culture, Spain. Survey about cultural participation in 2018–2019.

[2] DANE, Colombia. 2017 (available at Statista).

[3] Ministerio de Cultura de Argentina (available at Statista).

the UNESCO List. However, these have been included because there are well-known artists who are references to specific styles of music.

Nowadays, experiences are an important element in the value proposition of tourism companies and music is at the centre of some of these experiences. Examples can be observed in Airbnb, hotel chains, music record labels, tourism destinations and music festivals.

In the hospitality sector, experiences have been identified with the customer journey and the focus is combined with the hotel experience. These experiences involve the design of the hotel, facilities, front-line employees and other customers (Kandampully et al., 2018). However, in the sharing economy, studies have concluded that authenticity in the experience is perceived as a differentiation factor in accommodation services (Mody et al., 2019). Customers conceive authenticity as access to the local community that is people and culture (Li et al., 2019). Authenticity is a dimension of the Airbnb experiences identified in these studies. Mody et al. (2019) found that customers perceive better immersion experiences in the local community through Airbnb than through hotels.

Airbnb experiences are closely connected to the idiosyncrasy of countries. Experiences can be also found in Tripadvisor, although this website does not refer to them as experiences but as things to do or tours. The two websites offer music experiences centring on the Tango in Argentina, the fado in Portugal, reggae in Jamaica and flamenco in Spain. Customers can become immersed in local communities and live authentic and unique experiences (Li et al., 2019).

Music is at the centre of the value proposition in some hotel chains, which try to differentiate themselves from their competitors by creating a unique atmosphere. For example, the Hard Rock Hotel experience is based on rock music and Disney Hotels & Resorts offer Mariachi performances. The Universal Music Group record label is planning on opening some hotels with their own music venue in the United States, for experiences that might consist of a combination of hotels and festivals. All these are examples of the ability of resorts to disseminate current and past music, including the styles listed as intangible heritage by the UNESCO.

Some tourist destinations are associated with music, as is the case of Ibiza, in the Balearic Islands. Berrozpe et al. (2017) analysed the brand image of the island and found that the cultural dimensions perceived by people were related to electronic music. Music is present in the airport, hotels, beaches and discotheques. If we think about Jamaica as a destination, we probably think about Bob Marley and reggae music. When non-Spanish people think about Spain, they usually think about flamenco.

Festivals and live music concerts are one of the main offerings that destinations use to attract tourists as a means to transmit their intangible heritage. Festivals aimed at preserving and transmitting local heritage engage people from a community as well as involving audiences from other municipalities and countries who appreciate the significance of that heritage. For example, 600,000 participants attended the Buenos Aires Tango Festival in 2017.[4] Live music concerts have become an important activity

---

[4] Statista.

to transmit musical heritage. In Spain, live flamenco concerts were the second most popular type of concert in terms of attendance in 2019.[5] In Portugal, around 417,000 concertgoers went to live fado music concerts. This was equivalent to 2.4% of total live performance participants.[6]

All the examples presented in this introduction and those that are included in this book indicate how important music is for people across the world and how it engages them, offering many styles and degrees of involvement that can be adapted to everyone. This introduction has shown that music as intangible heritage and music as a business can go hand in hand, extending the opportunity for the former to become well known and making people more aware of the need to safeguard it.

References

Berrozpe, A., Campo, S., & Yagüe, M. J. (2017). Understanding the identity of Ibiza, Spain. *Journal of Travel & Tourism Marketing, 34*(8), 1033–1046.

FAO. (2016). *Free, prior and informed consent. Manual for project practitioners.* FAO, Rome. http://www.fao.org/3/I6190E/i6190e.pdf.

Fitterman Radbill, C. (2017) *Introduction to music industry: An entrepreneurial approach* (2nd ed.). Routledge.

Gonzaga Videira, T., & Martins Rosa, J. (2017). A new online archive of encoded fado transcriptions. *Empirical Musicology Review, 12*(3/4), 229–243.

IFPI. (2019). *Music listening 2019: A look at how recorded music is enjoyed around the world.* https://www.ifpi.org/resources/.

Instituto Nacional de Estatística. (2020). *Estatísticas da Cultura 2019.* INE, Lisbon. www.ine.pt/xurl/pub/71882171.

Kandampully, J., Zhang, T. C., & Jaakkola, E. (2018). Customer experience management in hospitality: A literature synthesis, new understanding and research agenda. *International Journal of Contemporary Hospitality Management, 30*(1), 21–56.

Li, J., Hudson, S., & So, K. K. F. (2019). Exploring the customer experience with Airbnb. *International Journal of Culture, Tourism and Hospitality Research, 13*(4), 410–429.

Mody, M., Hanks, L., & Dogru, T. (2019). Parallel pathways to brand loyalty: Mapping the consequences of authentic consumption experiences for hotels and Airbnb. *Tourism Management, 74*, 65–80.

Stoffel, A. M., & Victor, I. (2017). Museums and intangible cultural heritage in Lusophone countries. In M. Stefano & P. Davis (Eds.), *The Routledge companion to intangible cultural heritage* (pp. 426–440). Routledge.

UNESCO. (2009). *Evaluation of the nominations for inscription on the representative list of the intangible cultural heritage of humanity.* ITH/09/4.COM/CONF.209/13 Rev.2. UNESCO, Paris. https://ich.unesco.org/doc/src/ITH-09-4.COM-CONF.209-13-Rev.2-EN.pdf.

UNESCO. (2010). *Evaluation of the nominations for inscription on the representative list of the intangible cultural heritage of humanity.* ITH/10/5.COM/CONF.202/6. UNESCO, Paris. https://ich.unesco.org/doc/src/ITH-10-5.COM-CONF.202-6-EN.pdf.

UNESCO. (2011a). *Evaluation of the nominations for inscription on the representative list of the intangible cultural heritage of humanity.* ITH/11/6.COM/CONF.206/13 Add. UNESCO, Paris. https://ich.unesco.org/doc/src/ITH-11-6.COM-CONF.206-13+Corr.+Add.-EN.pdf.

---

[5] Data from Sgae 2019 (available at Statista).

[6] Instituto Nacional de Estadística (2020).

UNESCO. (2011b). *What is intangible cultural heritage?* UNESCO, Paris. https://ich.unesco.org/en/what-is-intangible-heritage-00003.

UNESCO. (2018a). *Basic texts of the 2003 convention for the safeguarding of the intangible cultural heritage, 2018 edition.* UNESCO, Paris. https://ich.unesco.org/doc/src/2003_Convention_Basic_Texts-_2018_version-EN.pdf.

UNESCO. (2018b). *Evaluation of the nominations for inscription on the representative list of the intangible cultural heritage of humanity.* ITH/18/13.COM/10.b+Add.2. UNESCO, Paris. https://ich.unesco.org/en/decisions/13.COM/10.B.18.

Open Access This chapter is licensed under the terms of the Creative Commons Attribution 4.0 International License (http://creativecommons.org/licenses/by/4.0/), which permits use, sharing, adaptation, distribution and reproduction in any medium or format, as long as you give appropriate credit to the original author(s) and the source, provide a link to the Creative Commons license and indicate if changes were made.

The images or other third party material in this chapter are included in the chapter's Creative Commons license, unless indicated otherwise in a credit line to the material. If material is not included in the chapter's Creative Commons license and your intended use is not permitted by statutory regulation or exceeds the permitted use, you will need to obtain permission directly from the copyright holder.

The Impact of the Music Industry in Europe and the Business Models Involved in Its Value Chain

Blanca de-Miguel-Molina, Rafael Boix-Doménech, and Pau Rausell-Köster

1 Introduction

The impact of creative and cultural industries can be analysed using different values, with the focus depending on the subject. From a cultural point of view, Addis and Rurale (2021) considered four values: the identity value, the economic value, the creative value and the well-being value. Applied to the music industry, the *identity value* is associated with its ability to create a community and its interest for both current and future generations. The *economic value* is related to the revenue streams the music industry generates, while the *creative value* refers to its ability to innovate. The *well-being value* of the industry is represented by the effect of music on our mental state and how we change the songs we listen to depending on the context. From the economic viewpoint, Oxford Economics, in its report for IFPI (2020b), measured the direct and indirect impact of the industry. According to this report, the industry employed a total of two million people in 2018. Direct impact accounted for 1.3 million employees and indirect impact for 0.7 million people. This chapter aims to focus on the industry's economic and creative value.

It presents the main data related to the importance of the music industry in Europe, including number of firms and employees. The region is a hub in terms of the amount

---

B. de-Miguel-Molina (✉)
Department of Business Organisation, Universitat Politècnica de València, Valencia, Spain
e-mail: bdemigu@omp.upv.es

R. Boix-Doménech
Departament D'Estructura Econòmica, Universitat de València, Valencia, Spain
e-mail: rafael.boix@uv.es

P. Rausell-Köster
Departament D'Economia Aplicada, Universitat de València, Valencia, Spain
e-mail: pau.rausell@uv.es

© The Author(s) 2021
B. de-Miguel-Molina et al. (eds.), *Music as Intangible Cultural Heritage*, SpringerBriefs in Economics,
https://doi.org/10.1007/978-3-030-76882-9_2

of music recorded and publishing activities, and as an innovative centre in the development of music streaming. The music industry involves many different activities in its value chain and there are different players in each of these activities. In this analysis, some of these activities were selected and the business models of companies engaging in these activities are explained. Some of the companies analysed included the Universal Music Group record label and the streaming services Spotify and Deezer. The study presents their business models, including their value proposition, revenue streams and their key resources, such as proprietary technology, which explain how they compete in their markets. We also aim to discuss the challenges posed by the digital impact on exhibition activities, and to do so, we have focused on opera houses in Europe. As cultural institutions, they are examples of the presence of the identity value and are important to transmit intangible cultural heritage. The opera houses included in the analysis are also examples of creative value as they have been able to adapt to changes in their sector.

2 The Impact of Music in Europe

This section focuses on the direct impact of the music industry on the European economy. The most recent analysis (IFPI, 2020b) estimated that the industry has a GDP multiplier effect equal to 2.2, which means that every euro in GDP generated by music creates an additional €1.20 in total GDP. The multiplier effect in recording activities shows a multiplier effect of 2.8. Therefore, every euro in GDP generated by music recording firms creates an additional €1.80. Moreover, the report estimated that the direct impact of the music industry on employment in Europe is around 1.3 million jobs. In 2019, the industry in Europe grew by 7.2%, led by the United Kingdom, Germany and France (IFPI, 2020a).

OECD data indicated differences between European countries in terms of the impact of recording and publishing activities on employees and enterprises (see Fig. 1). The greatest impact of these activities came from Germany, the United Kingdom, France and Sweden. In the publishing market, IMPF (2020) reported Europe to be the leading region by revenue in this activity (52.5% total revenue), followed by North America (25.6%) and Asia–Pacific (15.1%). However, these are only some of the music industry's activities. The total impact of the sector according to the European Commission was estimated at around 1,168,000 employees (European Commission, 2020).

The impact of culture can be explained by the budget households allocate to music activities (Eurostat, 2019). Cultural expenses can generate direct and indirect impacts. Directly, European households spend an average of 1.5% of their budget on music. There are, however, differences in the percentages for recorded music. For example, the figure stands at 3.8% in the Netherlands and 2.7% in the United Kingdom.

European citizens participate in cultural activities in which music is the central feature or an important element of the cultural offering, such as concerts and festivals.

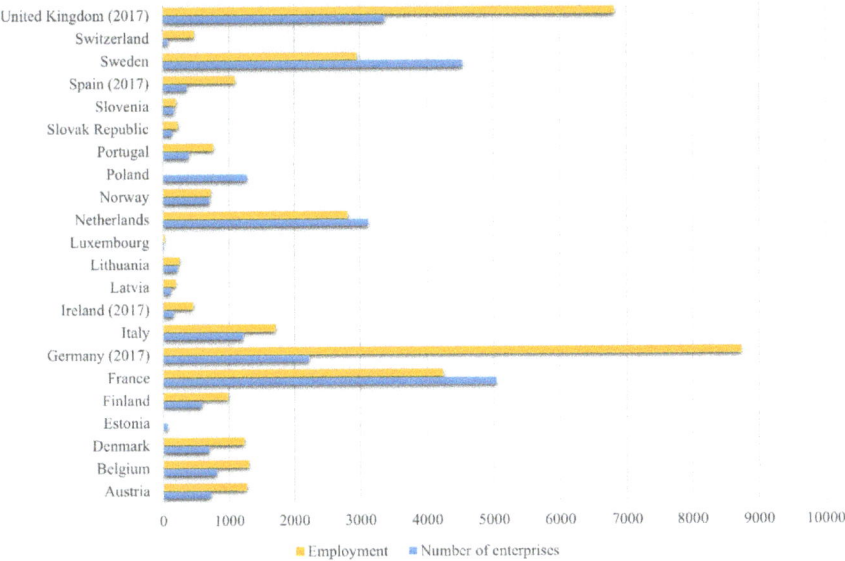

Fig. 1 Impact of sound recording and music publishing activities in Europe in 2018 (*Source* OECD.Stat)

Eurostat data indicated that 44.5% of people attended live performances (theatres, concerts and ballet), with the highest percentages coming from Finland (66.7%), Norway (62.5%) and the Netherlands (60.5%). The average price of music festival tickets in Europe from 2014 to 2018 was around €178 and the audience at a festival like Glastonbury in 2019 was 210,000 people (Statista). This data can explain why total spending on music events organised in arenas in 2018 was around €1,112 million (IQ Magazine, 2019).

In terms of indirect impacts, households spend around 2.4% of their budget on musical instruments (Eurostat, 2019). There are also differences between countries with households in Portugal spending around 6.4% of their budget on these cultural goods, while in Poland this figure rises to 10.9% of their budget. The impact also differs according to household income with the highest income correlating with the highest budget allocated to culture (Eurostat, 2017).

In the following sections, additional impacts will be analysed through the study of the business models pertaining to specific activities in the music industry.

3 Business Models in the Music Industry Value Chain

A business model has been defined as "how companies make money" (Chesbrough & Rosenbloom, 2002), "how enterprises work" (Magretta, 2002) and "how a firm conducts its business" (Fjeldstad & Snow, 2018). The use of business models to

Table 1 Elements of a business model

Osterwalder and Pigneur (2010)		Fjeldstad and Snow (2018)		Teece (2018)	
Value creation	Key resources, key activities, Key partners	*Value creation*	Activities, resources, economics	*Cost model*	Core assets and capabilities, core activities, partner network
Value delivery	Value proposition, channels, customer relationship	*Value proposition*	Product benefits, promised solution quality, connectivity and conductivity	*Value proposition*	Product and service, customer needs, geographies
Value capture	Revenue stream, cost structure	*Value appropriation*	Revenue mechanisms, protection mechanisms	*Revenue model*	Pricing logic, channels, customer interaction

Source Authors' own

explain how businesses compete has grown in recent years. Nowadays, there is knowledge about how business models operate (Casadesus-Masanell & Ricart, 2011) and the importance of connections between the elements of a business model (Osterwalder et al., 2020). There is also more information about what is needed to ensure the success of a business model, such as platform business models (Cusumano et al., 2019). To apply these concepts and explain company business models, authors in the management field have highlighted certain elements which include how value is created, delivered and captured (Teece, 2018). Table 1 presents these elements, with the value proposition being a crucial element, both in the business model and in terms of competitive strategy. As Michael Porter pointed out (Magretta, 2012), a good strategy starts with a unique value proposition. It indicates the offering of products and services, the customer segments which will be targeted for the offering, the channels through which the offering will meet the customers, and how the firm connects with the customer. This value proposition will determine the resources and activities needed to deliver it to customers but also the partners required to support the activities. The revenue model will be based on the value perceived by customers while profitability will also depend on the costs encountered through the activities performed.

The value chain of an industry describes "vertical stages from raw materials into finished goods, where each stage represents a different industry in which firms compete" (Rothaermel, 2019). The value chain in creative and cultural industries involves the different stages from a creative idea to the final customer, who is the audience of the cultural services (De Voldere et al., 2017). In the music industry, the value chain starts with the artists who create a song and finishes with the end

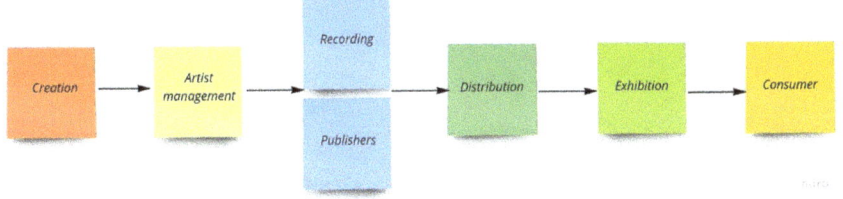

Fig. 2 The music industry value chain (*Source* Own elaboration from Rausell Köster and Montagut Marqués [2016] and De Voldere et al. [2017])

customers (Fig. 2). Recording activities refer to the sounds in a song while the publishing activity deals with the writing of the song. Therefore, the business model of music publishing firms is based on monetisation of songs, while the core of record labels' business model is monetisation from the song's recording (Simon, 2019). However, some record labels increase their revenue by including publishing. The distribution activity includes a player that has changed how music is listened to by new generations. In the exhibition activity, some organisations have had to deal with but have also taken advantage of digital transformation to reach current and new audiences.

When business models are considered, the value chain is not a linear system but "a system of interconnected activities which involves a firm, its customers, suppliers and partners" (Amit & Zott, 2021). In the music industry, companies compete with different business models depending on the activities they perform in the value chain. This chapter analyses the business models of organisations in recording, publishing, distribution and exhibition activities to obtain the main elements in their current business models.

3.1 Business Models in Recording and Publishing Activities

Revenue from recorded music amounted to $21.5 billion in 2019 MIDIA Research (2020), with three labels accounting for around 66% of worldwide market share (Music & Copyright, 2020). These labels are Sony Music Entertainment (19.9%), Universal Music Group (29.8%) and Warner Music Group (16.5%). The remaining market share (33.8%) is divided between a whole host of independent labels, which have increased their presence in recent years (WIN, 2018). According to IFPI (2020b) estimates, there are 7,400 firms in the recording market in the European Union and the United Kingdom. Market concentration of the three big labels differs between European countries. According to data,[1] in 2017, the three labels accounted for 85% of the market in Spain, 77% in the United Kingdom and 65% in the Netherlands. Figure 3 shows the market share for the leading recording and publishing companies,

---

[1] Midea and Worldwide Independent Network (obtained at Statista).

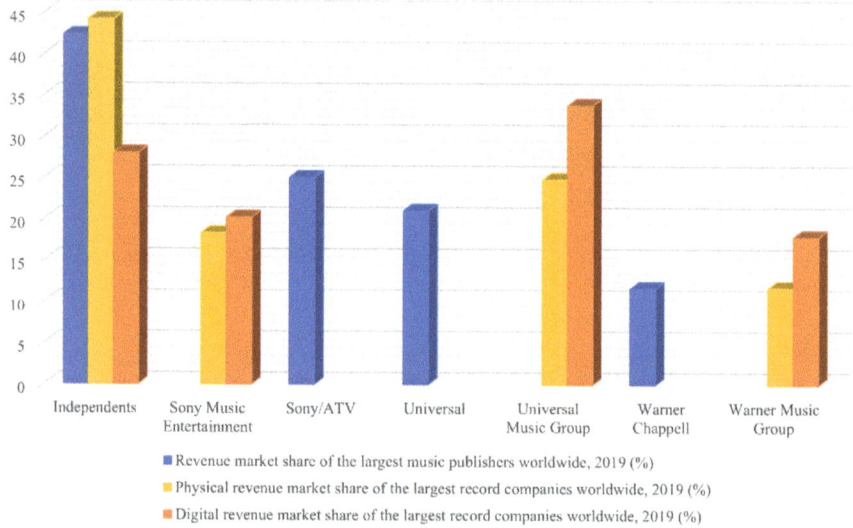

Fig. 3 Market share of music publishers and record companies worldwide, 2019 (*Source* Statista)

compared to the share of independent companies. The importance of the three largest record labels both in recording and in publishing is clear.

The business models of two European record labels are analysed in this section: the Beggars Group (United Kingdom) and Universal Music Group (Vivendi, France). An analysis of these record labels reveals they own more labels and have acquired even more in recent years. This growth strategy increases the concentration of market share in the hands of big labels as they have more resources to acquire other firms. Moreover, the expansion of labels also involves being a player in the music publishing industry. This strategy enables them to offer services to more artists but also increases the control of assets when negotiating for artists' revenue with other firms. However, revenue from publishing is lower than that obtained through recording, as explained for the two labels under study in the following paragraphs.

The Universal Music Group (UMG) label is owned by the Vivendi corporation and is also the owner of many other firms in the music recording and publishing markets. The label's recorded music revenue stood at €4,252 million between January and September 2020, with Europe being its second most important market (€1,231 million) after North America (2,123 million euros). Its publishing group (UMPG) has recently acquired Bob Dylan's catalogue of songs.[2] Music publishing generated €876 million for UMG from January to September 2020,[3] that is, 16.48% of music revenue. Other revenue streams from the music division are related to physical sales (€604 million, 11.37%) and merchandising (€105 million, 1.98%).

---

[2] https://www.umusicpub.com/uk/.

[3] https://www.vivendi.com/en/shareholders-investors/financial-publications-and-reports/financial-results/.

Streaming services, such as Spotify, are an important customer segment for record labels as they pay them for the songs listened to through their platforms. Vivendi indicated in its financial report that UMG's revenue increased during 2020 due to streaming. The label's music revenue amounted to €5,314 million from January to September, with €2,806 million coming from subscriptions and streaming (52.8%). Therefore, contracts with artists and their catalogue are key assets in their business models given that they offer them to streaming firms as part of their value proposition. Activities are centred on adding value to artists, and especially to those that increase the label's revenue. However, there is criticism over the impact of streaming on the rest of artists for whom revenue from platforms does not guarantee sustainable earnings (Mulligan, 2020b). In terms of the increased control exerted by labels over the music that is available to customers (Kask & Öberg, 2019), IMPALA, the association of independent music companies, estimated[4] that the three majors account for around 95% of the hits, dominating the market. This is because big labels have more people working for artists and make all the departments in the company available to them, including marketing, creative teams, press and publicity (IFPI, 2019).

The Beggars Group is an independent record label which owns[5] or has a shareholding in various independent labels, such as 4AD, Matador, Rough Trade, XL Recordings and Young Turks. In 2019, its revenue amounted to £37.7 million, according to the company's annual report.[6] The turnover analysis indicates that 82.8% of its revenue was obtained from sales and licensing of sound recordings, with 26.2% of them obtained in the United Kingdom and 73.8% in other countries. The Beggars Group also offers music publishing services. However, as an independent label, they do not have the infrastructure of the three big labels, so they need to be more innovative. Data from IMPALA indicates that independent music produces 80% of new releases. Moreover, the independent firms' strategy centres on specific genres, which might explain the higher percentage of artists that decide to renew their contracts with them (WIN, 2018). In some countries, however, this loyalty is higher, as is the case of Spain (97%), the Netherlands (93%) and Denmark (90%). On the contrary, loyalty is lower in other countries like Germany (68%), the United Kingdom (63%), France (48%) and Italy (41%).

In music publishing, firms protect songwriters, whose concern centre on the low rewards they receive from streaming services. According to MMF (2019), it is not a streaming issue but a question of too many participants in the royalty chain, each of them keeping a percentage of the value generated by the songwriter. Figure 2 indicates that big labels are also present in the publishing business, although independent companies are important in both recording and publishing activities. The main sources of revenue for publishing companies (IMPF, 2020) are television and radio (38.8%), live and background music (30%) and digital music (19%). Examples of independent firms in the publishing market are BMG and Kobalt.

---

[4] https://impalamusic.org/stats-2/.
[5] https://www.beggars.com/group/about.
[6] https://find-and-update.company-information.service.gov.uk/company/01414045/filing-history.

BMG is the music division of the German corporation, Bertelsmann. The division offers artists publishing, recording and audiovisual services and live performances. BMG has extended the services it provides to artists to give them a comprehensive offering. For example, they have included neighbouring rights, and in 2020, they acquired Undercover GmbH, to create a business unit for live music and events. They also included artist management in 2019. Its key resources are its staff (900 employees) and its proprietary technology, developed to improve customer transparency. Moreover, this technology also provides clients with data about the market, which helps them when making decisions. Deals with major artists are also an important key resource for BMG. Revenue from the division in 2019 was €600 million, 50% of which came from the United States and 16.6% from the United Kingdom.

Kobalt Music Group is an independent music firm which offers artists recording, publishing and neighbouring rights. In 2019, the firm's revenue amounted to $543.4 million, according to their financial report. This firm has also invested in proprietary technology, increasing transparency for clients and offering them personalised data about the market. According to Kobalt, this helps the firm to attract new clients and retain existing ones. The firm's key resource is its employees (650) and they mention the royalty collection societies as an important partner.

In conclusion, firms in publishing and recording activities base their business models on their clients, who are the artists. They upscale their business models extending the services they offer to each artist, to give them a comprehensive range of options. This also means the firms can grow their revenue streams. In the publishing market, companies have incorporated technology as an element in their value proposition that increases transparency for artists and provides data which is important to evaluate their business.

3.2 Business Models in Music Distribution

Streaming services have become an important player in the distribution business. According to data published by Statista (statista.com), worldwide revenue from streaming services amounted to €13,478.8 million in 2019. In the first quarter of 2020, streaming services had 400 million subscribers. In Europe, revenue amounted to €4,969.5 million in 2020, with 95.56 million users. This means Europe concentrates 36.9% of revenue and 23.9% of users. In the European market, there are general streaming platforms such as Spotify (Sweden, Luxembourg), Deezer (France), SoundCloud (Germany) and Tidal (Norway). There are also niche streaming services like Idagio (Germany), which is focused on classical music. The type of business model these platforms use is a freemium model, in which users select between free and premium subscriptions (Simon, 2019). Rivalry in the market is fierce as these platforms compete with the giant tech companies like Amazon, Apple and Google. Figure 4 shows that the impact of these competitors is greater in some countries than others, while in Scandinavia and France, the European streaming services are the most widely used.

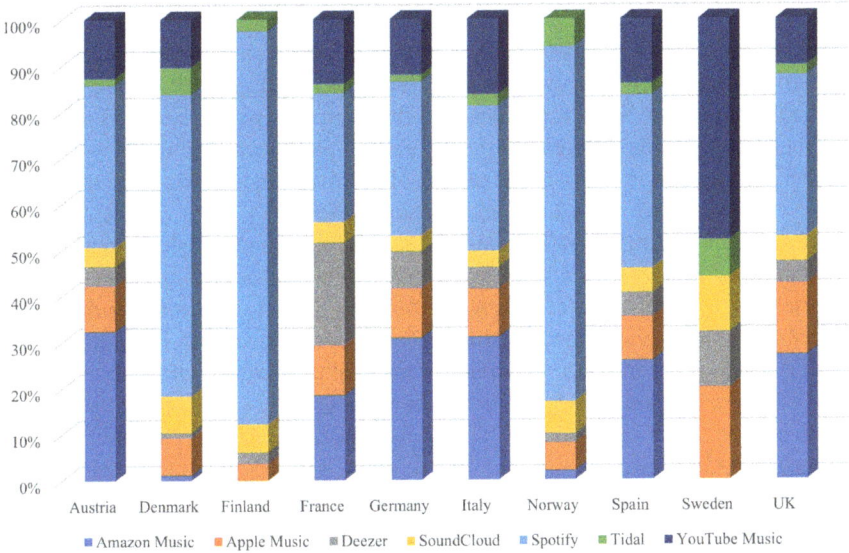

Fig. 4 Percentage of users by streaming service in Europe, 2020 (*Source* Statista Global Consumer Survey)

Section 3.1 details which streaming platforms are important customers for the record labels and which labels' revenue has increased thanks to these platforms. Streaming services have business models based on a two-sided platform, which require several factors to be and remain successful. Cusumano et al. (2019) cited the network effect, switching costs and multi-homing, the selection of profitable customers, entry barriers and being 'asset-light' as some of the elements included in these business models.

The *network effect* means that the platform needs users on both sides, i.e., artists and fans. Up until now, it has been easier to connect listeners than to attract artists. This explains why Spotify has created new services in an attempt to attract more artists to its platform. Its most recent strategy to appeal to artists has centred on partnering with a label, in this case, the Universal Music Group, and offering them new services. The results appear to be positive, according to Spotify's financial report. However, support from authors needs to give them a valuable service which can be converted into revenue.

With regard to *switching costs* and *multi-homing*, the lower the price of digital platforms, the greater the threat of multi-homing. This means that users are not loyal to one platform and they change from one to another or combine platforms simultaneously. As Vroom and Sastre Boquet (2019) pointed out, labels offer their catalogue to any platform that is interested and this restricts platforms' ability to differentiate their value proposition. Platforms need to offer additional services and improve the user experience to reduce the threat of multi-homing. They also need to try to increase switching costs for users by encouraging them to increase the amount of information they self-compile in their accounts, such as their playlists, for example. However, these elements can be easily copied by competitors, implying that platforms need to innovate continuously to offer differentiated services. Moreover, artists also use multi-homing to reach more fans and this increases rivalry between streaming services that try to be different, with the smallest platforms coming off worst. This rivalry increases when television streaming platforms include music-related products in their offering, such as concerts and documentaries.

The *selection of profitable customers* seems to be a complex task when we look at the platforms' financial results. We used Spotify and Tidal as examples, because they are more transparent with information, especially Spotify, as it makes information available through its website. Spotify's revenue amounted to €5,712 million from January to September 2020, which is greater than the revenue cited previously for UMG. However, Spotify obtained an operating loss of €224 million and a net loss of €456 million in the same period. Table 2 presents the impact of each user segment on the operating loss. Spotify had 144 million (43.8%) premium users and 185 million (56.2%) free users supported by advertisements. Therefore, premium users generated 91.9% of revenue while free users generated only 8.1% of turnover. As the cost of revenue plus operating costs amounted to €5,936 million, if costs are divided according to the revenue they generate, premium users would account for €5,455.2 million (91.9%) and free users for €480.8 million. However, if costs are divided by the number of users, the issue generated by free users becomes obvious, as Vroom and Sastre Boquet (2019) indicated. The firm's financial report reveals that free users increased more than premium users between 2019 and 2020, which could intensify the profitability issue. This confirms the advice given by Cusumano et al. (2019) about the importance of selecting profitable customers.

We also found data about the revenue obtained by other European streaming platforms.[7] In 2019, Deezer's turnover amounted to €331.08 million; Sound-Cloud earned $163.25 million; and Tidal's income was $109.89 million. Although their revenue is lower than Spotify's, the important factor in a business model is profitability. For example, Deezer had seven million subscribers in January 2019 (statista.com), representing around $47.3 dollars per user. Deezer, however, states it has 16 million active users, which would indicate more free users than premium users, and represents income of €20 per user.

Idagio, the niche classical music streaming service, has started to offer a free service although it offers limited access compared to the total value proposition. This could indicate that they are trying to attract more users, based on the theory that some of them will change to a premium option in future. This free option could also attract advertisement revenue. However, it could mean that they have not been able to expand as fast as they hoped, in line with analysts' studies about the impact of the current crisis on the number of premium subscribers (Mulligan, 2020a).

Another element cited by Cusumano et al. (2019) is *entry barriers*, which in this industry does not seem to be a major issue as new competitors are constantly entering the market. However, it seems that large amounts of funding are required to attract

---

[7] www.dnb.com.

Table 2 Measuring the profitability of a streaming platform (million €)

Users (type)	Revenue	Users (number)	Revenue by user (€)	Costs* (A)	%	Costs* (B)	%	Operating loss (A)	Operating loss (B)
Premium	5248 (91.9%)	144 (43.8%)	36.4	5,455.2	91.9	2,600	43.8	(207.2)	2,648
Free	464 (8.1%)	185 (56.2%)	2.5	480.8	8.1	3,336	56.2	(16.8)	(2,872)
Total	5,712	329	17.36	5,936	100	5,936	100	(224)	(224)

*Cost of revenue, R&D, Sales & Marketing, General & Administration
Source https://investors.spotify.com/financials/default.aspx

new users. In addition, the cost linked to paying recording and publishing companies is around 70% of revenue. Tidal offers a breakdown of how each euro from a user's subscription (https://tidal.com/whatistidal) is spent. In a premium subscription, which costs $9.99, the company pays $7.3 (73.07%) to recording and publishing firms for royalties and rights and $0.40 (4%) to credit card and transaction companies. Tidal keeps 23% of the user's subscription. The fee for a HiFi subscription is $19.99. 71% of this fee goes to recording and publishing firms, 2.5% goes to credit card and transaction companies, while Tidal retains 26.5%. Transactions through the App Store increase the user fee by $3 to $6. Data from Spotify also suggests payments of around 74%. Therefore, platforms need to develop proprietary technology while they design an *"asset-light" business model*. Technology ensures a premium experience for users and increases the services offered but involves very high investment.

In conclusion, streaming platforms have become an important player in music distribution but rivalry in the market is fierce and guaranteeing the profitability of their business models is a challenge.

3.3 Business Models in Exhibition Activities

Here, we analysed the business models of five opera companies located in five European cities: the Royal Opera House (London), La Scala (Milan), the Paris Opera, the Teatro Real (Madrid) and the Vienna State Opera to explain the main elements of each one. They were selected because they are examples of organisations that have managed to innovate while preserving their mission and cultural heritage.

Opera houses are located in historical buildings which have been the centre of social meetings for centuries. The Royal Opera House has been operating out of the Convent Garden theatre since 1858[8]; La Scala has been in its building since 1778[9]; the Paris Opera[10] inaugurated the Palais Garnier in 1875 and the Bastille building in 1989; the Teatro Real was founded in 1818[11]; and the Vienna Opera House was built in 1869.[12] Studies indicate that the building, the social interlinks and the quality of performances explain loyalty (Tubillejas-Andrés et al., 2020; Vigolo et al., 2019). Therefore, opera managers consider the atmosphere and the season they offer as important elements of their value proposition, connecting tangible and intangible cultural heritage.

The number of spectators attending opera performances is not high in general. For example, cultural statistics indicate that around 4% of the population in the United Kingdom and 3.3% in Spain attended an opera performance in 2019. This percentage

---

[8] https://www.roh.org.uk/about/the-royal-opera/history.

[9] https://www.teatroallascala.org/en/la-scala/theatre/history.html.

[10] https://www.operadeparis.fr/en/magazine/350-years/architecture/architecture.

[11] https://www.teatroreal.es/en/teatro-real.

[12] https://www.wiener-staatsoper.at/en/staatsoper/the-opera-house/history-architecture/#c4408.

represents 1,306,000 spectators in Spain[13] and 3,844,789 spectators in Germany.[14] How much revenue can an opera house obtain solely from attendance? We found data for 2019 about annual revenue for three of the theatres analysed,[15] but this information did not specify the source of the revenue. The total revenue obtained by the Fondazione Teatro alla Scala di Milano was $55.99 million; turnover at the Royal Opera House Convent Garden Foundation was $181.09 million and as the Wiener Staatsoper it stood at $59.57 million.

Are there differences in opera productions between European countries? According to the *Operabase* website (www.operabase.com/statistics), there are differences between opera houses in each country. In the 2019/2020 season, the most popular productions in Italy were *Aida* (Verdi), *Tosca* (Puccini) and *Carmen* (Bizet). In the same season in France, *Cosi fan tutte* (Mozart), *Rigoletto* (Verdi) and *Madame Butterfly* (Puccini) were the most performed works, while in Germany *Die Zauberflöte* (Mozart) and *Don Giovanni* (Mozart) headed the list. These differences could indicate that opera houses adapt their season to the audience's preferences but also that they tend to specialise in specific opera productions that can then be offered to other theatres.

It is important to consider that opera houses are based in historical buildings whose upkeep is expensive. They also need to pay employees' salaries, so the greater the number of activities they offer, the larger numbers of people they will need to perform them. To support[16] its theatres, the Italian government has allocated €182.8 million to opera foundations for 2021. Opera houses are also supported by firms and associations of opera friends. However, having these historical buildings as a base gives these firms the chance to rent out these spaces and host famous events. This is the case of the Wiener Staatsoper, which hosts the Vienna Opera Ball and the New Year's Concert. The opera orchestra is the Vienna Philharmonic. The Teatro alla Scala Foundation also rents out space in different pavilions to hold events.

The need for revenue streams explains why the value proposition of opera houses includes opera and other performing arts, such as concerts and ballet, thus enabling them to attract different audiences and diversify their revenue stream. Why is ballet a revenue stream for opera houses? It attracts an extra 5% of spectators to the theatre but more importantly, it appeals to young people. Data for cultural attendance in Finland, for example, reveals that 5% of people attended classic ballet performances in 2019, while attendance of the 'new generation' (10–14 years old, born after 2000) was 8%. Moreover, attendance of women in this generation was 13%. As theatres need to maintain their intangible heritage (a place where people meet over a period of decades) and transmit it to new generations, offering ballet performances and training is a good strategy. This option can boost opera house sustainability by attracting more community support. The Royal Opera House obtains revenue from activities for children in the mornings, and they also offer education to teachers.

---

[13] Ministerio de Cultura, Spain (Encuesta de Hábitos y prácticas culturales).

[14] German Theatre and Orchestra Association.

[15] www.dnb.com.

[16] Ministero dei Beni e delle Attività Culturali e del Turismo (Italy).

Opera companies and orchestras have been adapting their operations to the digital age as a way to keep their current audience and reach new ones. Kavanagh (2018) explained that some of these organisations have created their own record labels to keep control over this business segment so as not to have to resort to major record labels. The opera houses selected in this chapter offer video streaming of previous operas, concerts, dance performances and other shows. Although some theatres consider this technology as a source of revenue and charge fees to online audiences, others offer free streaming sessions. Opera houses started using social media as a first step in their digital transformation, followed by only selling tickets online. The Wiener Staatsoper also has an online shop focused on opera and it sells records and books. It also offers small screens in the theatre to every spectator so they can follow the subtitles, watch videos and receive other information about the performances. The Royal Opera House also has an online shop to buy other products, apart from tickets.

More recently, the opera houses analysed have introduced video streaming, though with some differences. Streaming became a revenue segment for the Royal Opera House before lockdown (including cinemas) and it kept an online channel open during the mobility restrictions imposed by the pandemic. It has used cinema, television and radio broadcasts to extend audiences in innovative ways. The Paris Opera offers performances through its platform for around €8. The Teatro Real has its own streaming platform, MyOpera Player, which it also makes available to other opera houses. It offers a yearly subscription model for €90 or a six-month subscription for €46. It also offers a non-subscription option, charging about €4 for each individual show.

In conclusion, opera houses are costly to maintain because they are located in historical buildings and because opera productions are expensive to stage. However, opera house managers and the teams analysed here have innovated to adapt their business models and find new revenue streams while preserving the intangible heritage associated with these institutions. The support of the private sector, governments and communities has helped them to ensure the resources and capabilities required to be able to adapt their business models to digital transformation.

4 Conclusions

This chapter has studied the impact of the music industry through the importance of the activities that make up the industry value chain. The business models of certain companies were analysed to obtain the main pointers on how firms compete in every segment of the value chain. The main conclusions can be summarised as follows:

The first conclusion is that the music industry generates a positive direct and indirect economic impact on European countries. The recording industry generates the biggest impact, with a multiplier effect of around €1.80 euros for every euro spent. Although this impact is greater in some countries, estimates indicate that the sector employs around 1,168,000 workers (European Commission, 2020).

The second conclusion refers to the business models adopted by recording and publishing firms. Recording is concentrated in a few big labels who rely on streaming services as an important customer segment. Their growth in recent years can be explained by services such as Spotify, which pays them for the songs listened to through its platform. In the publishing market, companies have focused on technologies that increase transparency in their relationships with artists.

The third conclusion is about streaming services, which concentrate around 24% of users in Europe. Although these services have been described as important customers for recording companies, their dependence on these labels has been pointed out as an important handicap for streaming platforms in terms of profitability. This is a major challenge for streaming services, which have focused more on increasing turnover than establishing profitability through their use of freemium business models.

The last conclusion is centred on the exhibition business through the example of opera houses. These cultural institutions have been able to innovate while preserving their mission and cultural heritage. As attendance at opera performances is not generally high, theatres have extended the number of products and services on offer to capture new revenue streams. These include ballet and training and, more recently, they have also added a digital strategy through streaming services. The difference with other cultural institutions such as museums is that opera houses have considered streaming as a source of revenue.

The music industry comprises many activities and actors that make it difficult to measure their total impact. This chapter has focused on some activities in the industry to indicate how stakeholders' business models influence their ability to generate impact and sustain it over time. A lack of data for some activities makes it difficult to evaluate their total impact, which explains why there are few studies which have attempted to measure their global effect.

References

Addis, M., & Rurale, A. (2021). A call to revise cultural business management. In M. Addis & A. Rurale (Eds.), *Managing the cultural business: Avoiding mistakes, finding success* (Chap. 1, pp. 1–31). Routledge.

Amit, R., & Zott, C. (2021). *Business model innovation strategy: Transformational concepts and tools for entrepreneurial leaders.* Wiley.

Casadesus-Masanell, R., & Ricart, J. E. (2011). How to design a winning business model. *Harvard Business Review, 89*(1/2), 100–107.

Chesbrough, H., & Rosenbloom, R. S. (2002). The role of the business model in capturing value from innovation: Evidence from Xerox Corporation's technology spin-off companies. *Industrial and Corporate Change, 11*(3), 529–555.

Cusumano, M. A., Gawer, A., & Yoffie, D. B. (2019). *The business of platforms: Strategy in the age of digital competition, innovation and power.* Harper Business.

De Voldere, I., Romainville, J. F., Knotter, S., Durinck, E., Engin, E., La Gall, A., Kern, P., Airaghi, E., Pletosu, T., Ranaivoson, H., & Hoelck, K. (2017). Mapping the creative value chains: A study on the economy of culture in the digital age. *European Commission*. Brussels. https://op.europa.eu/s/owDB. Accessed 14 December 2020.

Eurostat. (2017). *Culture statistics—Cultural participation*. https://ec.europa.eu/eurostat/statistics-explained/index.php?title=Culture_statistics_-_cultural_participation#Cultural_participation_by_income.

Eurostat. (2019). *Culture statistics, 2019*. Publications Office of the European Union.

European Commission. (2020). *Creative Europe: Monitoring Report 2019*. Publications Office of the European Union.

Fjeldstad, O. D., & Snow, C. C. (2018). Business models and organization design. *Long Range Planning, 51*, 32–39.

IFPI. (2019). *Global music report 2019*. IFPI. https://powering-the-music-ecosystem.ifpi.org/download/GMR_The_Value_of_a_Label.pdf.

IFPI. (2020a). *Global music report: The industry in 2019*. IFPI. https://www.ifpi.org/wp-content/uploads/2020/07/Global_Music_Report-the_Industry_in_2019-en.pdf.

IFPI. (2020b). *The economic impact of music in Europe*. Oxford Economics. https://www.ifpi.org/wp-content/uploads/2020/12/IFPI_music_in_Europe.pdf.

IMPF. (2020). *Independent music publishing global market view 2020*. http://www.impforum.org/impf-launches-independent-music-publishing-global-market-view-2020/.

IQ Magazine. (2019). *European arena yearbook 2019*. https://www.statista.com/statistics/783308/live-events-spend-by-genre-in-europe/.

Kask, J., & Öberg, C. (2019). Why "majors" surge in the post-disruptive recording industry. *European Journal of Marketing, 53*(3), 442–462.

Kavanagh, B. (2018). Reimagining classical music performing organisations for the digital age. In C. Dromey & J. Haferkorn (Eds.), *The classical music industry* (Chap. 9). Routledge.

Magretta, J. (2002). Why business models matter. *Harvard Business Review, 80*(5), 86–92.

Magretta, J. (2012). *Understanding Michael Porter: The essential guide to competition and strategy*. Harvard Business Review Press.

MIDIA Research. (2020, March 5). Recorded music revenues hit $21.5 billion in 2019. *MIDIA Research*. https://www.midiaresearch.com/blog/recorded-music-revenues-hit-215-billion-in-2019.

MMF. (2019). *The songs royalties guide*. https://themmf.net/site/wp-content/uploads/2019/05/mmf_songroyaltiesguide-1.pdf.

Mulligan, M. (2020a, June 3). *The global music industry will decline in 2020*. MIDIA Research. https://www.midiaresearch.com/blog/the-global-music-industry-will-decline-in-2020.

Mulligan, M. (2020b, November 27). *Time to move beyond the song economy*. MIDIA Research. https://www.midiaresearch.com/blog/time-to-move-beyond-the-song-economy.

Music & Copyright. (2020). *Total recorded music market share worldwide in 2019, by label*. https://www.statista.com/statistics/947107/recorded-music-market-worldwide-label/.

Osterwalder, A., & Pigneur, Y. (2010). *Business model generation*. Wiley.

Osterwalder, A., Pigneur, Y., Smith, A., & Etiemble, F. (2020). *The invincible company*. Wiley.

Rausell Köster, P., & Montagut Marqués, J. (2016). El valor del patrimonio musical valenciano. Una aproximación desde la economía de la cultura. In R. Marzal Raga (Coord.), *El valor cultural de la música. Punto de partida para el estudio del patrimonio música* (Chap. 14, pp. 183–192). Editorial Aranzadi.

Rothaermel, F. T. (2019). *Strategic management* (4th ed.). McGraw-Hill Education.

Simon, J. P. (2019). New players in the music industry: Lifeboats or killer whales? The role of streaming platforms. *Digital Policy, Regulation and Governance, 21*(6), 525–549.

Teece, D. J. (2018). Business models and dynamic capabilities. *Long Range Planning, 51*, 40–49.

Tubillejas-Andrés, B., Crevera-Taulet, A., & Calderon Garcia, H. (2020). Assessing formative Artscape to predict opera attendees' loyalty. *European Business Review*. https://doi.org/10.1108/EBR-10-2019-0273 (in press).

Vigolo, V., Bonfanti, A., & Brunetti, F. (2019). The effect of performance quality and customer education on attitudinal loyalty: A cross-country study of opera festival attendees. *Nonprofit and Voluntary Sector Quarterly, 48*(6), 1272–1295.

Vroom, G., & Sastre Boquet, I. (2019). *Spotify: Face the music*. IESE Case. IESE Publishing.

WIN. (2018). *WINTEL Worldwide independent market report 2018*. https://winformusic.org/wintel/.

Open Access This chapter is licensed under the terms of the Creative Commons Attribution 4.0 International License (http://creativecommons.org/licenses/by/4.0/), which permits use, sharing, adaptation, distribution and reproduction in any medium or format, as long as you give appropriate credit to the original author(s) and the source, provide a link to the Creative Commons license and indicate if changes were made.

The images or other third party material in this chapter are included in the chapter's Creative Commons license, unless indicated otherwise in a credit line to the material. If material is not included in the chapter's Creative Commons license and your intended use is not permitted by statutory regulation or exceeds the permitted use, you will need to obtain permission directly from the copyright holder.

The Role of Public Policies in Enhancing Cultural and Creative Industries: An Analysis of Public Policies Related to Music in Colombia

Flor Marleny Gómez-Reyes, Daniel Catalá-Pérez, and María de-Miguel-Molina

1 Introduction

The creative industries concept was first used in 1994, in Australia, when the *Creative Nation* report was published (UNESCO, 2013). However, its major impact came in 1997 when the Department of Culture, Media and Sports created the Working Group of Creative Industries in the United Kingdom (UNCTAD, 2010). Since then, the United Kingdom has been very active in spreading the idea of cultural and creative industries (CCIs) in the European Union. According to the United Nations, CCIs are those that *"create, produce and deliver products and services using intellectual capital as their main income"* (UNCTAD, 2008, p. 20) and they are of great importance for regional economic development, especially in developing countries (UNESCO Forum of Ministers of Culture, 2019).

The cluster concept has a long-standing tradition in literature (Cooke et al., 2006). Its central argument is that when similar competing businesses are located in the same district and share skills and ideas, enabling mutual inspiration (Islam, 2000), they are more effective. Clusters have been especially attractive in the creative and cultural industries (UNESCO, 2019). Concentrating CCIs in clusters can enhance their intellectual capital (Baculáková, 2018) because the core of knowledge is based on collective learning (Bialic-Davendra et al., 2016; UNCTAD, 2008). Moreover, CCI clusters can support SMEs (Zheng & Chan, 2014), which are the typical size of companies in this sector.

F. M. Gómez-Reyes (✉)
Universidad Tecnológica de Bolívar, Cartagena, Colombia
e-mail: fgomezr1@ucentral.edu.co

D. Catalá-Pérez · M. de-Miguel-Molina
Universitat Politècnica de València, Valencia, Spain
e-mail: mademi@omp.upv.es

© The Author(s) 2021
B. de-Miguel-Molina et al. (eds.), *Music as Intangible Cultural Heritage*, SpringerBriefs in Economics,
https://doi.org/10.1007/978-3-030-76882-9_3

CCIs tend to be concentrated in geographical areas which have the characteristics of a metropolitan area, such as large cities (Boix et al., 2011). In these areas, the local productive system is more concentrated and CCIs have a greater impact on economic activity. Bogota, Colombia's capital city, is an example of these geographical areas.

However, due to the different types of agglomerations associated with cities, three approaches can be applied to an analysis of CCIs in Bogota: pure agglomeration (geographical proximity), complex industry (minimising transaction costs) and/or social network (high levels of social integration). In this study, however, we focus only on a pure agglomeration analysis to assess the concentration of "hot spots" in a city, in line with Boix et al.'s (2011) study of 16 European cities.

In this analysis, the authors established four categories of clusters: (i) economies with low urbanisation, which are formed in isolation and are usually made up of specialised companies; (ii) high levels of polycentrism, with the formation of groups with similar specialisations that facilitate synergies; (iii) low levels of polycentricity and high urbanisation, centred on a single point in the city due to an urban structure whose orography does not allow expansion and benefits from complementarities; (iv) and polycentrism, which occurs in large cities when there is income speculation that causes a rise in revenue, making it difficult to concentrate clusters in one point. This environment encourages creative environments (Boix et al., 2011, p. 757).

The process of creating public policies goes through different stages: identifying and defining the problem, obtaining information, developing different alternatives, selecting the criteria to implement them and evaluating their results (Bardach, 1998). In the case of CCI policies, different international organisations and institutions agree that public intervention focuses on eight main areas: institutions and regulatory frameworks (to promote favourable conditions), information and knowledge (for continuous communication), human resources and learning (development tools), infrastructure (spaces for CCIs), financing (direct, indirect and self-sustainable), markets and population (satisfying demand through goods supply), cooperation (networks) and creativity and innovation (depending on the social and political context) (Organización de Estados Iberoamericanos, 2016).

In the area of cooperation and integration, the advocacy and strengthening of joint initiatives in the creative sector involve promoting creative districts (Organización de Estados Iberoamericanos, 2016, p. 159). Nevertheless, cooperation must go hand in hand with government measures to find sustainable financing and communication strategies to develop and encourage innovation, training and constant reskilling for CCI actors (Organización de Estados Iberoamericanos, 2016, p. 167).

Any policy on culture and creativity must include economic objectives such as equity, efficiency, a positive trade balance, economic development and full employment, to ensure positive impact on the well-being of consumers and CCI services. Furthermore, to obtain a good balance between supply and demand, sufficient quality production is necessary, enhancing creative processes and guaranteeing a culture of consumption of CCIs at national and international levels, as well as scenarios to reinforce diversity, design, own brand and connectivity (Organización de Estados Iberoamericanos, 2016).

Moreover, for clusters to be able to revitalise a sector, such as the music industry, there must be a governance model that generates success and sustainable competitiveness (Cooke & Lazzeretti, 2008). For example, during the recession of the 1970s, the governments of the United States and Western Europe developed strategies to regenerate their city centres through public policies to increase cultural and creative consumption (Binns, 2005).

2 Background

2.1 CCI Policies in Colombia and Bogota

In Colombia, cultural policies were introduced in the 1970s. In 1976, the Colombian Institute of Culture launched its first cultural development plan, "Cultural policy in Colombia", which included the cultural history of Colombia from its aboriginal cultures, the founding of cities, political independence through to the development of education and literature, and took in the country's cultural and natural heritage (Ruiz & Marulanda, 1976). From the 1980s onwards, different policies and regulations for CCIs and cultural support were developed: six from 1982 to 1989, nine from 1991 to 1997 and eight from 2000 to 2017.

CCI policies are currently included in the 2018–2022 National Development Plan (NPD) and, in 2019, a Vice Ministry of Orange Economy was created, under the Ministry of Culture. This NPD is also aligned with the United Nations' Sustainable Development Goals (SDGs) (UNESCO, 2019). Today, Colombia has divided CCIs into three areas and there are around 25 public policies for their improvement. As we can see (Fig. 1), there are three main areas for CCIs: arts and heritage (17 public policies), cultural industry (4 public policies) and functional creations or creative services (2 public policies). In addition, two crosscutting public policies are applied to the three areas.

Figure 2 shows that the main efforts have focused on the arts and heritage. However, this area only provides 28.3% of CCIs' added value[1] in Colombia, while the creative services area contributes 44.4% and cultural industries 27.3%. CCIs contributed 3.2% to Colombia's global economy in 2018 (DANE, 2019).

On the other hand, cluster policies have gained importance in Colombia since its Competitiveness Private Council (CPC) together with the International Trade Bank (Bancoldex), through its Development and Innovation Unit (Inpulsa), signed a cooperative agreement in 2013 to create a cluster network in Colombia. In the field of CCIs, this trend to promote clusters has been reinforced through the District

---

[1] Added value: "Additional value created by an economic agent through the production process. It is obtained from the difference between the value of production at basic prices and the value of intermediate consumption at purchase prices used by economic agents in their production processes" (DANE, 2019, p. 15).

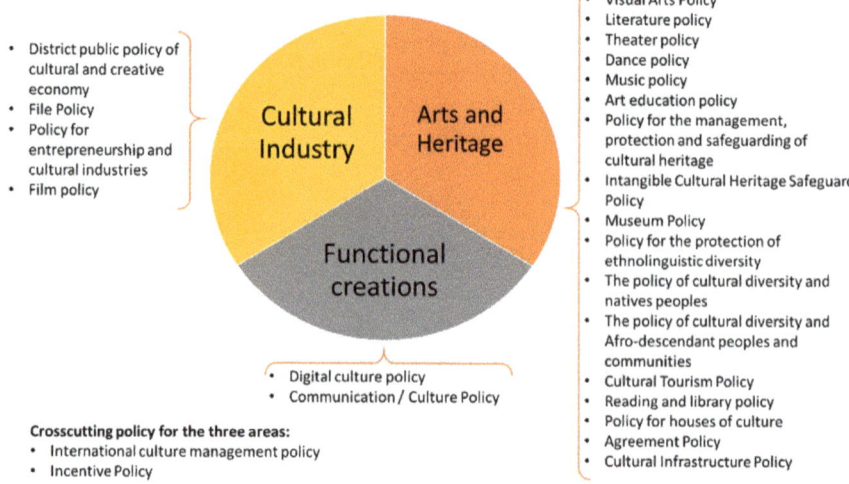

Fig. 1 Public policies by CCI area in Colombia (*Source* Authors' own based on data from the Colombian Ministry of Culture [2010])

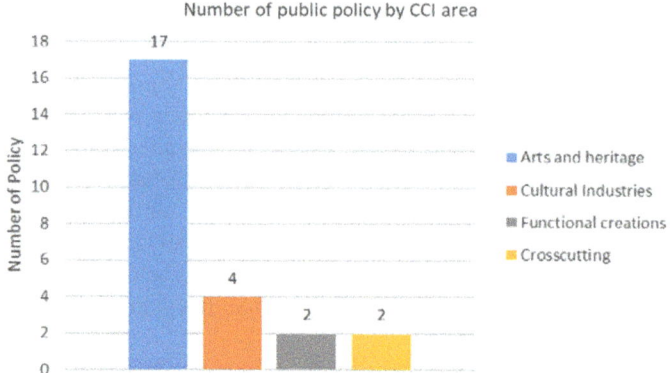

Fig. 2 Number of CCI policies by area (*Source* Authors' own based on data from the Colombian Ministry of Culture [2010])

Public Policy for the Cultural and Creative Economy included in the aforementioned cultural industry area of Colombian CCI policies.

Their general objective is to develop them through five strategic lines: (i) promotion of cultural industry products and services; (ii) improving access to financing mechanisms; (iii) supporting local initiatives for the development of cultural industries; (iv) expansion of specialised training; (v) and the promotion of new technologies in the development of business models for cultural industries (Conpes, 2019, p. 16). These lines are consistent with the areas of public intervention mentioned above proposed by the Organization of Ibero-American States (2016).

One of this local strategy's main objectives is to propose the creation of infrastructures to encourage stakeholder interaction, generating scenarios for the exchange of knowledge to enhance their creative processes, which should result in CCI implementation (Organización de Estados Iberoamericanos, 2016). For this reason, the national government, aligned with the Bogota Council, promoted the creation of a local cluster known as an ODA (Orange Development Area) focused on offering CCI-related academic programmes, given that in 2010, 32% of these types of academic training options were estimated to be inactive (Ministerio de Cultura, Ministerio de Comercio, & Planeación, 2010).

ODAs can be generated in two ways (Alcaldía de Bogotá, 2019): (i) induced as the result of public policies or government programmes, which aim to transform abandoned spaces and marginal areas into new drivers for social and cultural development (p. 25), (ii) and spontaneous as the result of economic activities linked to the cultural and creative economy that evolve spontaneously within the territory. These ODAs have a high density of cultural equipment and significant numbers of training courses related to the sector (p. 27).

2.2 CCI Policies Focused on Music in Colombia

In Colombia, music has historically been the way for different cultures to promote their cultural heritage from primitive communities to the present day. Music is conceived as part of communities' social development process (Ministerio de Cultura de Colombia, 2010). In 1982, Law 23 was published with the specific aim of protecting copyright and defending intellectual, heritage and cultural rights (Congreso de Colombia, 1982). This Law was modified in 2018 by Law 1915, adding other provisions related to copyright (Congreso de Colombia, 2018).

The artists in each region permeate their music and lyrics with their own individual hallmark given by cultural diversity. The music in each municipality and region describes their own local traditions, as well as the variety of different instruments that each region has. It depends on the natural inputs that the land provides to create it, as well as on the influence of the migrants who have settled in each region, bringing part of their own culture. Music has developed in Colombia within this mix of materials, culture and traditions (Ministerio de Cultura de Colombia, 2010). Thus, given this musical wealth, the government created the National Music Plan for Coexistence (PNMC), which considered the cultural and professional dimensions of the music production cycle.

In any case, the first musical policies and programmes in Colombia were implemented by the Ministry of National Education through the so-called *Colcultura*, an organisation created in 1968 whose objective was: "the creation, strengthening and projection of national symphonic groups (bands, choirs and symphony orchestras) and the management of operas and concerts at the Colón Theatre" (Ministerio de Cultura de Colombia, 2010, p. 139). Additionally, the CREA[2] programme was launched as "an expedition through Colombian culture" to locally disseminate the popular music of each of the country's regions.

From 1997 to 2002, with the creation of the Ministry of Culture, new music promotion policies were developed through the National Council for Economic and Social Policy (CONPES) (Ministerio de Cultura de Colombia, 2010, p. 139). However, it was not until 2006 that the budgets to ensure the sustainability of musical traditions increased substantially, with the "Guidelines for the strengthening of the National Music Plan for Coexistence".

This PNMC was established through the 2002–2006 National Development Plan and served as a guide for the mayors and governors of Colombia to promote education and musical practice at the municipal, regional and national levels. This plan linked training, research, infrastructure, entrepreneurship, financing and the coordination of public musical activities (Ministerio de Cultura de Colombia, 2010). The objective was to strengthen the musical heritage of each region and extend its outreach on the national and international markets. In this sense, the plan promoted national projects and initiatives at international level organised through multilateral organisations and cooperating countries (Ministerio de Cultura de Colombia, 2010, p. 51).

At national level, public entertainment was strengthened through Law 1493 passed in 2011, which sought to formalise the performing arts through instruments such as increased economic resources, tax incentives and the simplification of procedures for holding events (Ministerio de Cultura, 2011). Musical events are held in all regions of the country, with both the Pacific and Atlantic coast areas being rich in rhythms and musical creations. It is important to highlight that there are strongly rooted Afrodescendant and indigenous cultures on the coasts that still preserve their cultural and musical traditions, which date back to the time of the conquest.

The majority of musical production in the country, however, is in the large cities where industry is concentrated. Of a total of 599 companies dedicated to music, 37% are in Bogota, 16% are in the region of Antioquia and 13% in Valle del Cauca. It is important to note that the region of Antioquia is the only one in the country with its own Regional Music Plan (2014–2020), which has strengthened the music industry and the international outreach of musicians and singers.

Despite the formality of the rules and laws, piracy has been one of the hurdles for musical entrepreneurs. To combat this, in 2006, the Congress of the Republic approved Law 1032, which amended articles in the Colombian Penal Code to further tighten both prison and economic penalties for anyone engaging in illegal telecommunications activities, and violations of copyright and related rights (Congreso de la República, 2006).

Efforts to protect the music industry, especially in terms of copyright, are aimed at preserving the culture provided by music and at generating incentives that encourage more Colombian citizens to pursue a career in music. However, as shown in Fig. 3, only 599 of the 7,427 companies in the creative, artistic and entertainment sector belong to the music creation area, which represents only 8% of the total. Live musical

---

[2] The Crea Program is a strategy that is part of the District Development Plan 2020–2024.

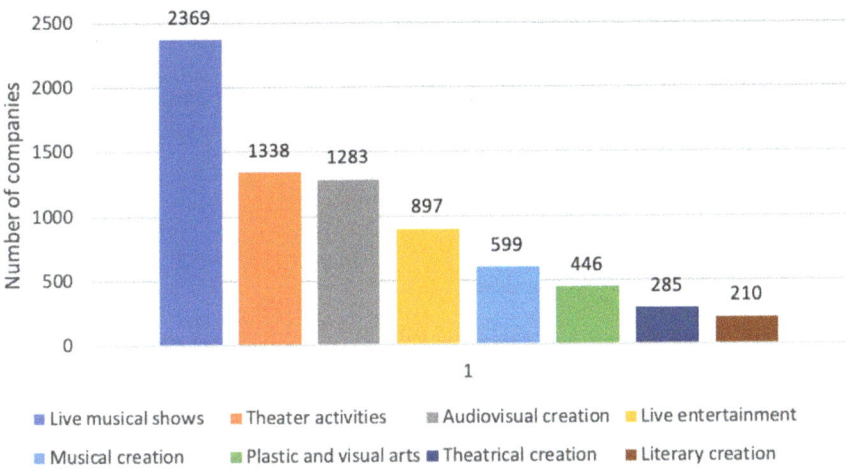

Fig. 3 Total companies that make up the creative, artistic and entertainment sector (*Source* Geoviewer Business Directory 2018 [DANE, 2018])

performance activities, meanwhile, represent 31% of all creative, artistic and entertainment activities, hence the importance of Law 1493 passed in 2011 on public performances in the country.

For Colombia, it is of vital importance to protect copyright given the high levels of informality that exist in the country. For this reason, since 1982, laws have been enacted and modified to protect Colombian authors and musicians. Likewise, as part of its instruments to motivate musical entrepreneurs, in 2004, Law 881 established guidelines to pay tribute to the great national artists who have created and conserved the country's musical heritage over the last 500 years (Congreso de Colombia, 2004).

3 Characterisation of CCIs in Bogota: Identifying Clusters

The methodology that we propose to analyse public policies aimed at enhancing the cultural and creative industries and their clusters, specifically in the music sector, is a descriptive study to identify their characteristics and elements and discover possible associations in terms of behaviour. It is an analytical research method, since our aim is to identify the features that characterise public CCI policies and CCI clusters, and ultimately establish relationships between them. The main sources of information used were secondary sources (texts, magazines, national and international documents) centring on establishing a relationship between CCI policy and cluster literature, as well as their implications in their environment.

We characterised CCI companies and clusters in Bogota by applying statistical and geographical techniques to the database of Bogota companies engaged in this sector (Méndez Álvarez, 2006). Thus, we identified 113,685 firms located in the 20

Table 1 Total number of CCI in Bogota by activity

CCI in Bogota: total and partial inclusion activities			
Area	Sector	No. companies	% Sector
Arts and heritage	Associative activities and regulation	17,311	41
	Manufacturing activities in the creative economy	13,226	31
	Arts education, culture and creative economy	5,732	13
	Heritage cultural material and immaterial	*3,265*	*8*
	Performing arts and shows	*2,243*	*5*
	Visual arts	811	2
Total number of arts and heritage companies		42,588	100
Industries cultural conventional	Editorial	22,773	78
	Audiovisual	4,959	17
	News agencies and other information services	739	3
	Phonographic	*738*	*3*
Total number of cultural industry companies		29,209	100
Creations functional, new media and software	Design	18,121	43
	Digital media and content software	15,441	37
	Advertising	8,326	20
Total number of functional creations companies		41,880	100
Total general companies in the CCI		113,685	

Source Authors' own based on DANE (2018)

city districts. Table 1 shows the total number of CCIs in Bogota, which are divided into thirteen sectors belonging to three main areas. Of the 113,685 existing CCIs, 42,588 belong to the arts and heritage sector, 29,209 to the cultural industry and 41,888 to functional creations.

A second step was to identify clusters. In the first place, we considered induced and spontaneous ODAs (Alcaldía de Bogotá, 2019). Thus, in 8 of the 20 districts in Bogota, 11 creative clusters were identified: nine created by citizens from a down-top perspective and two created by the national government from a top-down viewpoint. Figure 4 shows that the Chapinero district concentrated the largest number of conglomerates (4 of the 11). On the other hand, the two clusters promoted by the government are located in areas of Bogota that need regeneration to increase their economic development: Martires/Bronx and Fontibon.

The two ODAs created by the government have regenerated two parts of the city with complex social problems, such as drug addiction, prostitution, insecurity and

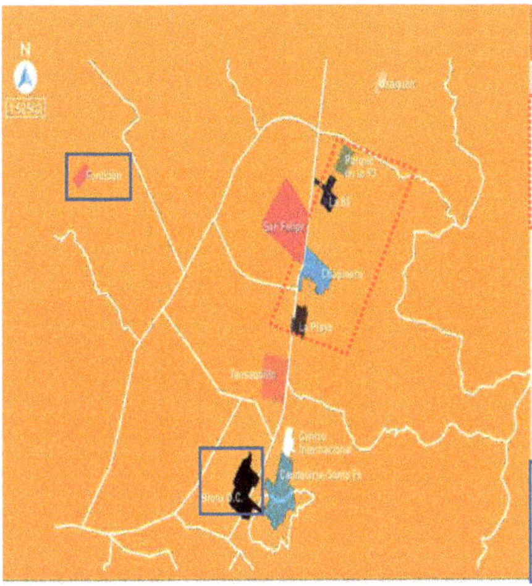

No.	Location	No.	Clúster	Created by
1	Usaquén	1	Usaquén	Market
2	Chapinero	2	Parque de la 93	Market
		3	La 85	Market
		4	Chapinero	Market
		5	La playa	Market
3	Barrios unidos	6	San Felipe	Market
4	Teusaquillo	7	Teusaquillo	Market
5	Santafé	8	Centro internacional	Market
6	La Candelaria	9	Centro histórico	Market
7	Mártires	10	Bronx D.C	National government
8	Fontibón	11	Fontibón	National government

Fig. 4 CCI clusters (ODAs) in Bogota D.C. (*Source* Authors' own based on the Secretariat of Culture of Bogota Alcaldía de Bogotá [2019])

violence (Gutiérrez & Sáez, 2018). In one of them, the government has created a techniques and technological education centre that offers artistic and cultural programmes, generating a process of urban revitalisation in these spaces (Harvey, 2015; Scott, 1997, 2010). Therefore, CCI policies and instruments focused on the development of collaborative spaces have helped to strengthen different CCI clusters in Bogota. In general, we can observe that public policies for CCIs have encouraged the development of clusters and the growth of CCIs in Bogota (Alcaldía Mayor de Bogotá, 2019).

4 Regional Public Policies with Emphasis on Music Industries

Public policies for the music industries are created by the Ministry of National Culture, but they are administered by individual regions in Colombia. Likewise, each region can issue its own public policies according to the characteristics of its own culture. In the particular case of Bogota, the implementation of public music policies is carried out through the District Institute of the Arts, whose objective is the promotion, strengthening and development of music from a human and artistic standpoint. Some of the public policy instruments focus on providing economic incentives, scholarships, awards, internships and artist residencies that promote the musical process in the city of Bogota, from the creation to the dissemination of musical projects (Ministerio de Cultura de Colombia, 2010).

In 2012, the UNESCO included Bogota in its network of "creative cities of music", a distinction earned by this city in recognition of its more than 70 music festivals, which have made Bogota the most important musical centre in Colombia regarding the culture satellite account[3] and the biennial culture survey (Secretaría de Cultura, 2012).

As shown in Table 2, public music policies have played a dominating role in adding economic value to the city of Bogota, where music has a total share of 4% in the area of conventional cultural industries and 18.3% in the area of arts and heritage. Thus, it contributes €92,527,750 to the total value added by the cultural and creative industries in the city of Bogota.

Table 2 demonstrates that music has an active role in two of the three cultural and creative industry areas. It has been strengthened as a result of public music policies and the instruments for their implementation.

5 Conclusions

The concept of cultural and creative industries has evolved since its inception, with music being one of the most representative sectors. Therefore, the importance of public policies centring on music for the promotion, strengthening and development of this sector in Colombia and, especially, in the capital city, Bogota, D.C., must be highlighted.

On the one hand, public policies can generate strategies to promote ODAs, for example, designing spaces, eliminating bureaucracy, improving managerial and entrepreneurial skills, and improving financial support. On the other hand, they are essential to promote the consumption of cultural and creative products and services (Rius-ulldemolins et al., 2016).

As shown in the clusters identified in some Bogota districts, CCI clusters promote knowledge which is transmitted and absorbed (Boix et al., 2015). Moreover, there are opportunities to create more ODAs in another 12 districts (Conpes, 2019). To do this, the Bogota local government published a guide offering recommendations to apply the model. Furthermore, a specific "Creative Economy" area has been created inside the Secretary of State of Culture to develop more public policies.

However, the political instability in Colombia may have an impact on the future of these policies given that CCIs are the flagship project of the current government. This means that its opponents associate CCIs with a political party and not an economic point of view.

Finally, the importance of music in Bogota D.C. has been recognised by the UNESCO for its contributions to adding economic value to the cultural and creative industries in Colombia. These advances have been achieved thanks to the creation, development and implementation of public policies that facilitate the musical growth

---

[3] The satellite account will help to assess the economic contribution of cultural industries and activities to GDP (UNESCO, 2009, p. 35).

Table 2 Added value of the cultural and creative industry in Bogota D.C.

Area	Value added 2018	%	Sector	Value added 2018	%
Creations functional, new media and software	€1,841,562,250	61.3	Digital media and content software	€1,094,849,500	59.5
			Advertising	€592,381,750	32.2
			Design	€154,331,000	8.4
Total number of functional creations companies				€1,841,562,250	100
Industries cultural conventional	€821,324,500	27.8	Audiovisual	€514,125,750	62.6
			Editorial	€215,693,250	26.3
			News agencies and other information services	€55,725,000	6.8
			Phonographic	*€35,780,500*	*4.4*
Total number of cultural industry companies				€821,324,500	100
Arts and heritage	€309,990,250	10.9	Arts education, culture and creative economy	€155,291,250	50.1
			Associative activities and regulation	€66,619,750	21.5
			Performing arts and shows	*€30,803,500*	*9.9*
			Manufacturing activities in the creative economy	€29,342,500	9.5
			Heritage cultural material and immaterial	*€25,943,750*	*8.4*
			Visual arts	€1,989,250	0.6
Total added value of arts and heritage				€309,990,000	100
Total added value CCI in Bogota D.C.				€2,972,876,750	100

Source Authors' own based on DANE (2018)

of the capital city of the country, making Bogota a hub for the world's largest musical shows and concerts.

Due to the above and given the potentialities of music at cultural, social and economic level for the city and therefore for the country, there is a primary need to continue creating and strengthening public policies and instruments for the development of Bogota and the Colombian music industry.

References

Alcaldía de Bogotá. (2019). Guía Práctica para la Creación de Áreas de Desarrollo Naranja. In *Política Pública Distrital de Economía Cultural y Creativa* (Secretaria). Bogotá. https://www.culturarecreacionydeporte.gov.co/sites/default/files/guia_practica_para_la_creacion_de_areas_de_desarrollo_naranja.pdf.

Baculáková, K. (2018). Cluster analysis of creative industries in the regions and districts of Slovakia. *Theoretical and Empirical Researches in Urban Management; Bucharest, 13*(3), 74–89. https://search.proquest.com/docview/2095705499?accountid=28445.

Bardach, E. (1998). *Los ocho pasos para el análisis de políticas públicas*. Grupo Editorial Miguel Ángel Porrua.

Bialic-Davendra, M., Bednář, P., Danko, L., & Matošková, J. (2016). Creative clusters in Visegrad countries: Factors conditioning cluster establishment and development. *Bulletin of Geography: So-Cio-Economic Series, 32*(32), 33–47. https://doi.org/10.1515/bog-2016-0013.

Binns, L. (2005). *Capitalising on culture: An evaluation of culture-led urban regeneration policy*. https://arrow.tudublin.ie/futuresacart.

Boix, R., Hervás-Oliver, J. L., & De Miguel-Molina, B. (2015). Micro-geographies of creative industries clusters in Europe: From hot spots to assemblages [Article]. *Papers in Regional Science, 94*(4), 753–772. https://doi.org/10.1111/pirs.12094.

Boix, R., Lazzeretti, L., Hervàs, J. L., & De Miguel, B. (2011). Creative clusters in Europe: A microdata approach. Valencia, Editorial ERSA. *New Challenges for European Regions and Urban Areas in a Globalised World*, 1–33.

Colombian Ministry of Culture. (2010). Cultural Policy Compendium. In *Colombian Ministry of Culture*. http://www.mincultura.gov.co/areas/fomento-regional/Documents/Compendio-Políticas-Culturales.pdf%5Cn. http://www.mincultura.gov.co/ministerio/politicasculturales/compendio-politicas-culturales/Paginas/default.aspx.

Congreso de Colombia. (1982). Ley 23. Diario Oficial (1982). http://derechodeautor.gov.co:8080/documents/10181/182597/23.pdf/a97b8750-8451-4529-ab87-bb82160dd226.

Congreso de Colombia. (2004). Ley 881 De 2004. https://www.funcionpublica.gov.co/eva/gestor normativo/norma_pdf.php?i=12916.

Congreso de la República. (2006). Ley 1032 De 2006. 2006 Diario Oficial § (2006). http://www.sec retariasenado.gov.co/senado/basedoc/ley_1032_2006.html#:~:text=Incurrir%C3%A1%20en%20prisi%C3%B3n%20de%20cuatro%20(4)%20a%20ocho%20(8,1.

Congreso de Colombia. (2018). Ley 1915. Diario Oficial (2018). http://es.presidencia.gov.co/normativa/normativa/LEY%201915%20DEL%2012%20DE%20JULIO%20DE%202018.pdf.

Conpes, D. C. (2019). *Política Pública Distrital De Economía Cultural Y Creativa 2019–2038*. Editorial Departamento Nacional de Planeación.

Cooke, P., & Lazzeretti, L. (2008). *Creative cities, cultural clusters and local economic development* (P. Cooke & L. Lazzeretti, Eds.). Edward Elgar.

Cooke, P., Martin, R., & Asheim, B. T. (2006). *Clusters and regional development: Critical reflections and explorations* (P. Cooke, R. Martin, & B. T. Asheim, Eds.). Routledge.

DANE. (2018). Departamento Nacional de Estadística. Geoportal, Directorio de empresas. https://geoportal.dane.gov.co/geovisores/economia/directorio-estadistico-de-empresas/?lt=4.456007353293281&lg=-73.2781601239999&z=5.

DANE. (2019). *Economía Naranja Segundo reporte 2019*. https://www.dane.gov.co/files/investigaciones/pib/sateli_cultura/economia-naranja/presentacion-rp-2do-reporte-economia-naranja-2014-2018.pdf.

Gutiérrez, C. A. B., & Sáez, F. A. A. (2018). La producción de marginalidad urbana: El proceso socio-histórico, emergencia y configuración del Bronx en Bogot [The production of urban marginality: The sociohistorical process, emergency and configuration of the Bronx in Bogot]. *IMAGONAUTAS*, 107–128.

Harvey, D. (2015). Od menedżeryzmu do przedsiębiorczości: transformacja procesu rządzenia miastami w późnym kapitalizmie z wprowadzeniem Boba Jessopa. *Zarządzanie Publiczne, 3*(3(33)/2015), 84–106. https://doi.org/10.15678/zp.2015.33.3.06.

Islam, F. (2000). *Socioeconomy of innovation and entrepreneurship in a cluster of SMEs in emerging economies*. Emerald Insight. https://doi.org/10.1108/10595421011047451.

Méndez Álvarez, C. E. (2006). *Metodología, diseño y desarrollo del proceso de investigación con énfasis en ciencias empresariales* (Limusa Nor).

Ministerio de Cultura. (2011). *Ley 1493 de espectaculos públicos*. https://www.mincultura.gov.co/areas/artes/ley-de-espectáculos-publicos/Documents/Ley_1493_2011.pdf.

Ministerio de Cultura de Colombia. (2010). *Compendio de políticas culturales*. https://www.mincultura.gov.co/ministerio/politicas-culturales/compendio-politicas-culturales/Documents/compendiopoliticas_artefinalbaja.pdf.

Ministerio de Cultura, Ministerio de Comercio, I. y T., & Planeación. (2010). D. N. de. Política nacional para la promoción de las industrias culturales en Colombia (Documento Conpes 3659). Departamento Nacional de Planeación. https://culturayeconomia.org/blog/documento-conpes-3659-politica-nacional-para-la-promocion-de-las-industrias-culturales-en-colombia/.

Organización de Estados Iberoamericanos. (2016). *Estudio comparativo de cultura y desarrollo en Iberoamérica*. https://oibc.oei.es/otros_documentos/Estudio_CD_OEI.pdf.

Rius-ulldemolins, J., Arturo, J., & Arostegui, R. (2016, March). *Treinta años de políticas culturales en España*.

Ruiz, J. E., & Marulanda, V. (1976). *La Política cultural en Colombia*. https://unesdoc.unesco.org/ark:/48223/pf0000134155?posInSet=1&queryId=90be9687-99ec-4bb5-9c96-d1efb87084ac.

Scott, A. (2010). Cultural economy and the creative field of the city. *Geografiska Annaler Series B-Human Geography, 92B*(2), 115–130. http://apps.webofknowledge.com.ezoris.lib.hokudai.ac.jp/full_record.do?locale=en_US&errorKey=&page=1&qid=16&log_event=yes&viewType=fullRecord&SID=U11efa4WINjqZNnH3Jy&product=WOS&doc=9&search_mode=DaisyOneClickSearch.

Scott, A. J. (1997). The cultural economy of cities. *International Journal of Urban and Regional Research, 21*(2), 323–339. https://doi.org/10.1111/1468-2427.00075.

Secretaría de Cultura, R. y D. (2012). Bogotá es Música | Secretaría de Cultura, Recreación y Deporte. Retrieved November 19, 2020, from https://www.culturarecreacionydeporte.gov.co/es/areas-de-trabajo/practicas-artisticas/musica.

UNCTAD. (2008). *Creative economy report 2008*. https://unctad.org/en/Docs/ditc20082cer_en.pdf.

UNESCO. (2009). 2009 UNESCO Framework for Cultural Statistics. In UNESCO Institute for Statistics (Vol. 5). http://www.uis.unesco.org.

UNCTAD. (2010). *Creative economy report 2010*. Switzerland.

UNESCO. (2013). *Creative economy report*. http://academy.ssc.undp.org/creative-economy-report-2013.

UNESCO. (2019). *Culture 2030 indicators*. UNESCO.

UNESCO Forum of Ministers of Culture 2019. (2019). UNESCO website: https://en.unesco.org/themes/protecting-our-heritage-and-fostering-creativity/forum-of-ministers-of-culture-2019.

Zheng, J., & Chan, R. (2014). The impact of "creative industry clusters" on cultural and creative industry development in Shanghai. *City, Culture and Society, 5*(1), 9–22. https://doi.org/10.1016/j.ccs.2013.08.001.

Open Access This chapter is licensed under the terms of the Creative Commons Attribution 4.0 International License (http://creativecommons.org/licenses/by/4.0/), which permits use, sharing, adaptation, distribution and reproduction in any medium or format, as long as you give appropriate credit to the original author(s) and the source, provide a link to the Creative Commons license and indicate if changes were made.

The images or other third party material in this chapter are included in the chapter's Creative Commons license, unless indicated otherwise in a credit line to the material. If material is not included in the chapter's Creative Commons license and your intended use is not permitted by statutory regulation or exceeds the permitted use, you will need to obtain permission directly from the copyright holder.

Soundcool: A Business Model for Cultural Industries Born Out of a Research Project

Nuria Lloret-Romero, Jorge Sastre-Martínez, Crismary Ospina-Gallego, and Stefano Scarani

1 Introduction

The world has changed and with it, jobs, tools and transportation. In 2007, 76% of schools in the USA had to ban mobile phones (Obringer & Coffey, 2007). Unfortunately, in 2019, there was still no official protocol to deal with the situation, sending contradictory messages to students (Dennen & Rutledge, 2019). Mobile phones need to be part of education, as they are a part of life. Schools have to harness the potential of technology in the classroom to address the digital divide (Scarani et al., 2020) and give students the skills they need in today's connected world (OECD, 2015).

Moreover, the current pandemic has had an enormous impact on global education, with more than 1.3 billion learners being unable to go to school (Hagan, 2020). In order to ensure the continuity of learning, educational institutions have embarked on setting up technological platforms to deliver online learning programmes to students. These include the Soundcool system.

Soundcool is a free system for musical, sound and visual collaborative creation through mobile phones, tablets and other interfaces. It consists of a set of modules such as virtual instruments, players (audio and video), live audio (microphone) and video (camera), audio and video effects, and mixers that work on Mac and PC computers. Soundcool modules are opened from the app and can be interconnected with each other. For example, a sound source, such as a virtual instrument and a microphone, can be connected to a delay effect, which is applied in real-time to that source. The main advantage of Soundcool is that these modules can be controlled via users' mobile phones or tablets, enabling collaborative creation, with both educational and professional applications.

N. Lloret-Romero (✉) · J. Sastre-Martínez · C. Ospina-Gallego · S. Scarani
Universitat Politècnica de València, Valencia, Spain
e-mail: nlloret@upvnet.upv.es

The app was designed to create audiovisual content between two or more people, although there have been times where 100 people have intervened in a particular artistic project. This means that all users can give their ideas at the same time to create audiovisual content under the supervision of a main computer operator who mixes the elements. The system is intuitive and very easy to use; for example, when children use it, they do not need instructions about controls, they just learn by constructing the project.

1.1 Opportunities Afforded by the Soundcool System

Soundcool has applications in fields like education, special needs education, music performances, artistic performances, dance and therapy for people with special needs and for patients with neurodegenerative diseases. It started out as a tool to complement music performances, but music teachers quickly saw the potential of the app for musical education. It has had successful results in this area, with at least 40 schools working with the tool and 6,000 monthly downloads. Thanks to the implementation of audiovisual content, Soundcool can now also be used in other subjects such as science, maths and languages, and it could also be interesting for other arts.

Soundcool is suitable for users with special needs, and the app is available for functional diversity schools. For example, the HoloLens glasses opened the door to dance schools, ballet companies and their performances. Research is currently underway on the possibilities of using the system for people with neurodegenerative illnesses, like Alzheimer's and Parkinson's.

1.1.1 Education

The educational part of Soundcool was developed by a team of doctors in pedagogy, UPV members, professionals in the performing arts and technology experts. Children and young people like the system very much because it speaks the technological language of their generation and they intuitively understand it without the need for instructions. As all the students participate in the project, they feel part of it, are motivated, kept busy and concentrated, which holds class discipline together.

The value of the system is that it enables children to explore different abilities, embracing multiple intelligence (Gardner, 1993) and giving them the opportunity to learn from their strong points. The key to Soundcool is that what kids construct through information comes through creativity and not from learning content off by heart.

In addition, the system uses resources that are available to many individuals in many educational centres, such as PC and Mac computers, microphones, webcams and speakers. The mobile phones and tablets used were selected because they are widely available among students and their families, eliminating the need for schools to acquire them.

1.1.2 Training for Teachers

Conversely to students, teachers need to be well informed about the system's possibilities to make the most of the tool. Soundcool has free online training in the shape of two MOOCs (Massive Open Online Courses): "Musical creation with Soundcool: Introduction" and "Soundcool 2: Video modules and creative proposals", available on edX, the international online course platform. Moreover, these course videos are also on the project's YouTube channel. These courses are endorsed by UPV certificates and they benefit teachers in terms of new educational technologies and methodologies, which also improves their resume.

1.1.3 Online Learning

Soundcool also facilitates collaborative creation with the app for distance education (Sastre et al., 2020). Some artistic experiences took place during lockdown with users being able to participate in artistic projects from home. These included:

- Collaborative project in the 21st Century International Festival.
- Seoul International Computer Music Festival, during which a collaborative piece was played with online participants from around the world.
- Presentation of collaborative creation with Soundcool for online education (Sastre et al., 2020), in the Korean Electro-Acoustic Music Society's Annual Conference.
- Online course to train teachers on musical and audiovisual collaborative creation projects in times of social distancing with Soundcool.

1.1.4 Special Needs Education

Soundcool was also adapted by the special needs educational team working with the performing arts and technology so it can be used for students with functional diversity. All the Soundcool tools are adapted to people who are blind, deaf, autistic or have other intellectual disabilities. It also gained funding to develop two projects related to this type of education which are described in the financial section.

After the experience of working with this community, it is important to highlight that this technology has improved aspects related to the users' psychomotor skills, their cognitive stimulation, improvements in social relations and well-being, increased self-esteem and the enhancement of each user's own abilities in the musical project (Briceño et al., 2014).

This technology could benefit countries where there are inclusion programmes, which means that children with special needs are in the same classroom as students without them, embracing diversity. Unfortunately, teachers are not trained in functional diversity. Out of 194 countries analysed, there are only six (three of which are Latin American) which have inclusive education laws, catering for all students. They are Chile, Colombia, Italy, Luxembourg, Paraguay and Portugal (Llorente, 2020).

1.1.5 Movement

Soundcool goes beyond the finger-eye movement functions used by the majority of apps. The research group introduced improvements in the app which involve using it with body movements instead of controls on the telephone. This encourages users to move around and explore other virtual experiences (Flavián et al., 2018). This part of the app started with Kinect, but after production of the device was halted, it continued its transformation to augmented reality and has recently evolved to virtual reality (Neira, 1993), i.e. an immersive multi-sensory experience (Gigante, 1993).

The Kinect is a camera-based sensor, primarily used to directly control computer games through body movement. The Kinect tracks limb and body position without the need for handheld controllers or force platforms. The use of a depth sensor also enables the Kinect to capture three-dimensional movement patterns (Galna et al., 2015).

The Kinect was used to adapt Soundcool to functional diversity students, specifically blind students, enabling them to use the app (Herrero et al., 2018). More adaptations were made, such as accessories and other tools, so that other special needs users could access Soundcool. Unfortunately, production of the Kinect stopped (Willson, 2017) and another alternative had to be found.

The alternative found was the HoloLens, which is an untethered mixed reality device that delivers an immersive experience. Users can see the reality and space around them through the HoloLens glasses, but also can see and touch a hologram of the Soundcool controllers in the same space, enabling them to move around, dance, create and have fun with the app. The only problem of the HoloLens is the price tag of $3,500 per unit (Microsoft, 2020) which makes it unfeasible for commercial purposes.

Given the price of the HoloLens glasses, a cheaper option was found in virtual reality. Users do not see the space around them, they only see what the glasses show them, but this modification reduces the budget to €200 for the virtual reality device.

In spite of the mixed reality and virtual reality, these developments have not replaced the functions of Kinect in terms of usability for blind people. Nevertheless, it has opened the door to other areas such as games, dance, ballet and degenerative illnesses.

1.1.6 Performance Art

The app started as a technological complement for professional musicians, but the research group has continued to create different activities to extend the content and options available on the system. It has also released artistic works to give visibility to the app and open the doors to participation in music festivals, and artistic and technology shows, where artistic collectives come together and network.

The most significant production is the multimedia opera *La Mare dels Peixos* (The Mother of Fishes), a free adaptation of a story by Enric Valor, with music by Jorge Sastre and Roger Dannenberg. Soundcool is ideal for music schools because it can be played by an orchestra of young musicians and singers, with the help of less than 10 professional musicians, which makes the performance affordable and interesting. The Soundcool part can be played by new students because they do not need to read music or play an instrument. The set is very simple and choreographies can be created by a group of children. This idea enabled a large number of students to participate in the musical show which was performed at the Palau de les Arts in Valencia (Spain) twice, in Mexico City with the Monterrey Institute of Technology and in Pittsburgh (USA) in 2020.

In the professional field, Soundcool has been used in festivals such as the Sonar Electronic Music Festival in Barcelona (Spain) and the Kikk Festival in Namur (Belgium). Other works have been presented, such as *Floating in the Deep Blue* for percussion and Soundcool live electronics and narrator.

An event that gave Soundcool a lot of visibility among artists was *El Guerrer de la Valltorta*, a circus showpiece that had an enormous band of musicians and electronic effects which was created with the app using over 100 devices. This event brought 4,130 music students together from 193 musical societies who, besides taking part in the show, were introduced to the Soundcool system.

1.1.7 Neurodegenerative Illnesses

Soundcool's new project seeks to work with people with neurodegenerative diseases and the team has already won funding for two projects to study the benefits of the system for this group (see Annex).

The first project consists of alternative therapies based on new audiovisual technologies for neurodegenerative diseases in times of social distancing due to COVID-19. Its aim is to promote preparatory actions to support the exploration and formulation of future research projects, looking for innovative scientific and technical memory through the UPV's Fisabio and Polysabio programmes. The other project centres on new music and audiovisual technologies to treat neurodegenerative diseases. This project has received a grant to consolidate AICO research groups.

2 Sustainability of the System

Up until now, Soundcool has been a non-profit project. It has been forged in the UPV, thanks to the willingness and generosity of the teachers and students that have worked on the initiative. Soundcool's most valuable asset is its highly qualified team, the majority of whom are teachers from the UPV and other universities that are part of the performing arts and technology research group. Most of the teachers are doctors in their field and contribute to the system in different ways. Some use the tool to improve the quality of their lessons, others write papers, others give ideas and time, leading to product innovations, some organise conferences that give visibility to the app, some bring contacts that can offer advice, and some let the group know about public tenders (see Annex).

For university lecturers, participating in this kind of projects brings a range of benefits including helping in the development of society, building credibility and prestige within the scientific community and society, and the chance to obtain funding for researchers. In addition, the UPV benefits by increasing its scores in world rankings, opting at possible subsidies for its research institutes, providing evidence of the productivity of the institution and future economic benefits (Lameda et al., 2015).

The UPV has scholarships for students that work in the research group or link their studies to benefit the group. These are available for graduate, Master and doctoral programmes. In graduate programmes, students carry out small projects and help in daily tasks; in the Masters' programmes, they perform small projects, and the PhD students normally go the extra mile to improve the system or use it in a different way (Ospina, 2019).

Other sources to pay for the team come from public tender awards to spend on research projects (see Annex). The Spanish Youth Job Scheme helps young people to access the job market, the Spanish Ministry of Employment pays some young people to help research and business, and these kinds of projects enable Soundcool to pay developers (Spanish Ministry of Employment, 2020).

There are all kinds of public tender awards available (see Annex). Some consist of money to spend on the project, some offer opportunities to test the product, others help with visibility and advice from experts on the matter, but most of them provide tools to continue developing related projects and new ways to explore the tool.

3 Conclusions

This paper details the entire process followed to create the Soundcool app. It explains opportunities in different markets and economic fields such as education, music performances, artistic performances, dance and therapy for special needs people and patients with neurodegenerative diseases.

Soundcool has been a non-profit project since the beginning, but now has a tight budget and lack of staff. If the app is to continue in the future, it needs to incorporate a business model supported by clients, so it can offer more, improved content in the platform in the long term.

The system is trying to be sustainable by developing a business plan with the help of experts in the UPV. It has recently entered the Co-lab Las Naves initiative, which is an incubator programme that aims to help the system reach the next level and hopefully start to sell the product in the midterm. Soundcool has carried out market research, market analysis and financial analysis in the field of education, which is the most developed part of the app, and the results are very promising.

Annex

a. *Awards*

NEM Art Prize 2017, for European creative industries from the New European Media association.

SIMO Education Award 2016, Technology for Teaching Hall, for the best experience in programming and robotics.

UPV Social Council Award in the category of University Social Responsibility for its work with ICTs and functional diversity.

The Orange Foundation Award for Accessibility and Personal Autonomy for the **Best Final Project** "Analysis, Design and Development of Virtual Reality Applications for the Rehabilitation of Children with Mobility Issues". Dr. Jorge Sastre, the project's Director, received the **Bankia Award** for Musical Talent in the Valencian Region as **Best Researcher**.

Bankia prize in the Best Musical Education Project category: "ExperimentArts: music, creativity and collaborative learning".

The system has been presented in numerous international publications, festivals, conferences and courses, as shown on the official website http://soundcool.org.

b. *Financing*

The Daniel & Nina Carasso Foundation. The objective of the project is the development of the visual part of Soundcool®, the implementation of apps for mobile devices to make it a free tool, the promotion of the use of the application in primary, secondary and music schools, and the development of its use for functional diversity.

(CulturArts) 2016, 2017, 2018. Grants for performances related to Soundcool®: the opera *La Mare dels Peixos* (Spain) and *The Mother of Fishes* (Mexico), the theatrical version of the opera, HoloSound and other events.

European Project KA1 Erasmus + : Collaborative Creation and Creativity through Music" 2017–1-ES01-KA101-036693, European Commission, 2018–2019. The objective of this project was to train music teachers to harness technology to design musical learning spaces where students become the creators of their own musical productions through the use of smartphones without the need for previous professional musical training.

European Project Erasmus + KA201 Technology at the service of learning and creativity: weaving European networks through collaborative music creation 2015–1-ES01-KA201-016139, European Commission, 2015–2017. This project was directed by Elizabeth Carrascosa and involved the strategic association of three centres in Spain and four centres in different European countries. During the 2015–2017 school years, these centres worked on creating different interdisciplinary activities via collaborative musical creation and video-creation using Soundcool®. The project included student exchange, the recording of a DVD and the publication of methodological guides for the tool.

European Project Erasmus + KA105 Music & Technology 2017–2-IT03-KA105-011802, European Commission 2017. The project involved different training activities with Soundcool® and other applications in eight countries. They included a concert which offered a sample of electronic music made with Soundcool® and a small concert offered by the Banda Contesse of Messina which also incorporated effects using Soundcool®.

Telefónica UPV Chair, 2017. This co-financed the development of a technological demonstrator for the Soundcool® OSC App for mobile devices, collaborating in the acquisition of Android and iOS mobile devices and other expenses.

Valencian Regional Government, 2015–2016. Soundcool: New Technologies for Music Education and Sound Creation AICO/2015/120. This project dealt with the development of the audio part of Soundcool® and the preliminary work focused on people with functional diversity.

Spanish Ministry of Education, Culture and Sports, 2013. New Technologies and Interfaces for Education and Production in Electronic Music PRX12/00557, Salvador de Madariaga Scholarship for research visits of senior professors and researchers in foreign centres, specifically for Jorge Sastre with Roger Dannenberg's Computer Music Group in the Computer Science Department at Carnegie Mellon University (Pittsburgh, USA).

Nuevas Tecnologías Audiovisuales e Interfaces para la Educación en Música y Creación Sonora, PAID-05–12-SP20120470. This project developed the basic modules for the first developments of Soundcool®.

References

Briceño, M., Hernández, C., Kelber, K., & Wolf, D. (2014). Musical creation and music therapy in users with intellectual disabilities. INTED Congress. Valencia.

Dennen, V., & Rutledge, S. (2019, July). Social media use in high school settings: Rules, outcomes, and educational opportunities. *SMSociety 19, Proceedings of the 10th International Conference on Social Media and Society, 205–213.*

Flavián, C., Ibañes, S., & Orús. C. (2018, July). The impact of virtual, augmented and mixed reality technologies on the customer experience. *Journal of Business Research, 100*, 547–560.

Galna, B., Barry, G., Jackson, D., Mhripiri, P., Olivier, L., & Rochester, B. (2015). Accuracy of the Microsoft Kinect sensor for measuring movement in people with Parkinson's disease. *Gait & Posture, 39*(4), 1062–1068.

Gardner, H. (1993). *Multiple intelligences: New horizons in theory and practice.* Basic Books.

Gigante, M. A. (1993). Virtual reality: Definitions, history and applications. *Virtual Real*, 3–14. https://doi.org/10.1016/B978-0-12-227748-1.50009-3.

Hagan, C. (2020, April 29). *1.3 billion learners are still affected by school or university closures, as educational institutions start reopening around the world.* UNESCO.

Herrero, C., Sastre, J., & Briceño, M. (2018). Technological platform Soundcool® and functional diversity: a proposal for inclusive learning and the promotion of creativity. *12th International Technology, Education and Development Conference.* https://doi.org/10.21125/inted.2018.0753.

Lameda, C., Suárez, L., Uzcátegui, R., & Zambrano, C. (2015). Importance of publishing scientific articles from individual, organizational and societal perspectives. *Redip, 5*(4), 914–927.

Llorente, A. (2020, June 23). *Inclusive education: Which are the 5 countries in the world that have laws promoting it (and two are in Latin America).* BBC News, Section Mundo.

Microsoft. (2020). *The ultimate mixed reality device.* https://www.microsoft.com/en-us/p/holoLens-2/91pnzzznzwcp/?activetab=pivot%3aoverviewtab.

Neira, C. (1993). Virtual reality overview. *SIGGRAPH 93 Course Notes 21st International Conference on Computer Graphics and Interactive Techniques, Orange County Convention Center*, Orlando, FL.

Obringer, S. J., & Coffey, K. (2007). Cell phones in American high schools: A national survey. *Journal of Technology Studies, 33*(1), 41–47.

OECD. (2015). *Students and learning: Making the connection, PISA.* OECD Publishing.

Ospina, C. (2019). Live music in Spain: Surviving between excess of regulations. *Aus Art., 7*(2), 91–102. https://doi.org/10.1387/ausart.21142

Sastre, J., Lloret, N., Scarani, S., Dannenberg, B., & Jara, J. (2020). Collaborative creation with Soundcool for socially distanced. Conference KEAMSAC2020, Seoul, Korea.

Scarani, S., Muñoz, A., Serquera, J., Sastre, J., & Dannenberg, R. (2020). Software for interactive and collaborative creation in the classroom and beyond: An overview of the Soundcool software. *Computer Music Journal, 43*(4), 12–24.

Spanish Ministry of Employment. (2020). *Garantia Juvenil.* Government of Spain. https://www.sepe.es/HomeSepe/Personas/encontrar-trabajo/Garantia-Juvenil.html.

Willson, M. (2017). *Exclusive: Microsoft has stopped manufacturing the Kinect.* Fast Company. https://www.fastcompany.com/90147868/exclusive-microsoft-has-stopped-manufacturing-the-kinect.

Open Access This chapter is licensed under the terms of the Creative Commons Attribution 4.0 International License (http://creativecommons.org/licenses/by/4.0/), which permits use, sharing, adaptation, distribution and reproduction in any medium or format, as long as you give appropriate credit to the original author(s) and the source, provide a link to the Creative Commons license and indicate if changes were made.

The images or other third party material in this chapter are included in the chapter's Creative Commons license, unless indicated otherwise in a credit line to the material. If material is not included in the chapter's Creative Commons license and your intended use is not permitted by statutory regulation or exceeds the permitted use, you will need to obtain permission directly from the copyright holder.

Breaking the Gender Gap in Rap/Hip-Hop Consumption

María Luisa Palma-Martos, **Manuel Cuadrado-García**, and **Juan D. Montoro-Pons**

1 Introduction

Although music has been around for thousands of years, we are still far from knowing what exactly attracts us to it, as Schäfer and Sedlmeier (2010) stated. Literature has recently shown abundant research into the issue of music consumption and preferences, and this has been complemented by official reports about participation in both live and recorded music.

In this regard, live concert attendance for rap/hip-hop music, which is one of the non-mainstream music genres, has increased in recent years, specifically by 1.3% since 2010, according to the 2018–2019 Survey of Cultural Habits and Practices (SCHP) conducted by the Spanish Ministry of Culture and Sport. This is followed by electronic, hard rock and jazz music, although attendance in these genres decreased slightly between 2014 and 2018. According to the same survey and in relation to gender, alternative music genres, especially rap/hip-hop, electronic and hard rock, seem to attract more male spectators to live music concerts. Specifically, over 5% of men and over 3% of women attend rap concerts.

When it comes to recorded music, listening to alternative genres is higher than concert attendance and figures are similar across these alternative genres (over 12%), namely electronic music, blues, jazz and rap/hip-hop. In this case, more men listen to non-mainstream music genres than women. Men prefer electronic music, rap/hip-hop, blues, soul and jazz while women prefer blues, soul, jazz, reggae, electronic music and rap/hip-hop. Figures for the latter increased for both genders from 2014 to 2018, by 6% for men and 3% for women.

M. L. Palma-Martos (✉)
Universidad de Sevilla, Sevilla, Spain
e-mail: mpalma@us.es

M. Cuadrado-García · J. D. Montoro-Pons
Universitat de València, Valencia, Spain

© The Author(s) 2021
B. de-Miguel-Molina et al. (eds.), *Music as Intangible Cultural Heritage*, SpringerBriefs in Economics,
https://doi.org/10.1007/978-3-030-76882-9_5

In 2018, 25.8% of free downloads were rap/hip-hop music versus 20% and 15% of electronic music and reggae, respectively. In terms of gender, 31.8% of men downloaded rap/hip-hop as opposed to 18.4% of women. This last figure is higher than other downloads made by women such as reggae (15.5%) and electronic music (13.8%) but is considerably lower than blues and soul (63.3%) and jazz (58.7%).

Finally, in digital service subscriptions, the same survey (SCHP, 2018–2019) shows that 23% of subscribers listen to rap/hip-hop, very closely followed by electronic music with 22.6%, and other genres (under 18%). A breakdown of rap/hip-hop listeners on these platforms shows that the 23% total was made up of 28.5% of men and 17.4% of women. However, female subscribers listening to this type of music was the highest percentage in comparison with other minority genres such as blues (17.2%), electronic music (16.2%) and reggae (14.6%).

Previous data show different gender-related consumption patterns in the case of minority music genres. Music consumption, including differences by gender, has been studied in different academic disciplines. In psychological research, some studies have analysed the influence of gender on music preferences. In this regard, men seem to prefer rebellious music (i.e. heavy metal and punk music) while women choose easy listening music (i.e. pop and country music) (Colley, 2008; George et al., 2007; Zweigenhaft, 2008). Similarly, following North (2010) and Herrera et al. (2018), men show greater preferences towards more aggressive, exciting music styles, linked to behavioural disconformity with social rules. Conversely, women prefer softer music, with more emotional content, made to dance to and with clear dependence on social media patterns (Colley, 2008). Although Colley (2008) stated that the underlying structure of music preferences is not necessarily the same, women show higher preferences for unpretentious music (Bonneville-Roussy et al., 2013). In this regard, Langmeyer et al. (2012) also found gender differences: men are mutually exclusive in their music preferences, whereas women are more likely to overlap. This is in line with what Crowther and Durkin (1982) stated in relation to greater musical eclecticism in the female gender. Finally, when analysing social identity and gender, Tipa (2015) noted that women usually listen to music in many of their daily activities, while for men, music plays a major role in social and affective relationships between peer groups.

The sociological approach highlights that women participate more than men in highbrow cultural activities (Bihagen & Katz-Gerro, 2000; Dimaggio, 1982; Lizardo, 2006), which is linked to early socialisation in arts and socioeconomic status (Bourdieu, 1984; Collins, 1988; Lizardo, 2004), the labour market and marital status. In addition, omnivorous consumer behaviour is associated with individuals that possess higher levels of human, economic and cultural capital, regardless of gender (Christin, 2012; García-Álvarez et al., 2007; Katz-Gerro & Osullivan, 2010; Peterson, 1992; Peterson & Kern, 1996). In the economic literature, Prieto-Rodriguez and Fernández-Blanco (2000) showed that gender (being female) and education (upper secondary or university degree) are predictors of omnivorous music consumption. However, this has a negative effect in the case of popular music (Favaro & Frateschi, 2007; Montoro-Pons & Cuadrado-García, 2011).

This paper, focused on rap/hip-hop consumption, aims to gain a deeper insight into the role of gender participation in this popular music genre. Specifically, we aim to test the existence of gender differences in its consumption and appreciation. In doing so, we first summarise the literature review on music consumption in relation to rap/hip-hop. Then, the exploratory research undertaken is described. This is followed by a results and comments section and ends with a discussion.

2 Rap/Hip-Hop Consumption Literature

The consumption of rap/hip-hop has been discussed, both directly and indirectly, from different standpoints. These mainly centre on three academic disciplines: psychology, sociology and marketing (consumer behaviour). The psychological perspective has dealt with social identity, personality and perceptions, among other variables. In terms of social identity, Dixon et al. (2009, p. 355) focused on an ethnic group (black people and immigrants), analysing their collective self-esteem within the community. Three findings can be noted from this work. First, "African American audience members' collective self-esteem was positively related to their consumption of rap music (viewers who consumed more rap videos also had a higher sense of collective self-esteem)". Second, black consumers with strong Afro-centric features, viewing videos with Afro-centric standards of beauty instead of Euro-centric ones, increased their identification. Finally, they stated that: "participants are able to use their cultural lens and ethnic identification to identify rap content which can potentially empower them". These findings are consistent with prior research focused on black audiences (Allen, 2001; Appiah, 2004). These studies point to the importance of race in relation to the rap music genre with theories possibly differing for white individuals. This is in line with what others think of hip-hop music because of its connection to race, class, sexism and black culture (Jacobson, 2015; Rose, 2008). While rap may be used to create new identities for relatively small numbers of white and Asian urban music enthusiasts, for most black urban music enthusiasts, this music is more likely to reflect and consolidate already existing racial identities (Tanner et al., 2009). In this sense, "hip-hop contributes to the understanding and construction of race, thereby contributing to racial formation theory that maintains the stratification with whites privileged above nonwhites" (Jacobson, 2015, p. 847).

Personality has also been related to music. Several theories support the link between personality and music preferences, specifically its uses and the gratification approach (Rosengreen et al., 1985). In this regard, people prefer styles of music that reinforce and reflect aspects of their personalities and personal identities (Rentfrow & Gosling, 2007). In addition, according to the model of optimal stimulation (Eysenck, 1990; Zuckerman, 1979), people tend to choose the type of music that moves them towards their optimal arousal level. In particular, Rentfrow and Gosling (2003) found that people who enjoy intense styles of music, such as rock, heavy metal and punk (rap/hip-hop could also be included) score high on psychological measures of thrill-seeking and openness. They also value freedom and independence. These authors, who determined the major dimensions of music preferences and their association with the Big-Five personality factors, also found that the fourth dimension (energetic and rhythmic), defined by rap/hip-hop, soul/funk and electronic/dance music, was positively related to extraversion and agreeableness, flirtatiousness, liberalism, self-perceived attractiveness and athleticism but negatively related to social dominance, orientation and conservatism. Bonneville-Roussy et al. (2013) also found that preferences for rap/hip-hop were positively associated with sociability, status orientation and physical attractiveness.

Music preferences and interpersonal perceptions have also been studied, bringing relevant findings. For instance, MacNamara and Ballard (1999) found that individuals with high resting arousal and antisocial characteristics preferred arousing styles of music that centred on a rebellious theme such as heavy metal, rock and rap. On the other hand, Rentfrow and Gosling (2006, p. 239) showed that "extraversion was positively related to music attributes such as energy, enthusiasm, and amount of singing and the genres country and hip-hop". In summary, the relationship between music preferences and personality may vary for different groups based on factors such as geography and age (Zweigenhaft, 2008).

Delsing et al. (2008, p. 128) focused their research on teenagers' music preferences revealing that adolescents who liked urban music (which includes rap/hip-hop), as well as pop and dance music, tended to score relatively high on extraversion and agreeableness. This was related to extravert desires to mingle with peers and to have fun. The authors stated that this could be explained by the model of optimal stimulation. This study also provides support for the generalisability of Rentfrow and Gosling's (2003) four-factor structure of music preferences across cultures and age groups. In later studies, Rentfrow et al. (2011) provided a model of musical preferences based on listeners' affective reactions to excerpts of music from a wide variety of musical genres, based on five factors. Urban music was largely defined by rhythmic and percussive music (rap, funk and acid jazz) in this case. They concluded that the music model was free of genre and reflected emotional/affective responses to music. Preferences were influenced by both social connotations and specific auditory features of music. A new study by Rentfrow et al. (2012) confirmed that preferences for music are also determined by specific musical attributes.

The sociological perspective states that rap/hip-hop is dominated by male artists and focuses mainly on a male audience, which commonly drives to hypermasculinity, misogyny, demeaning women, and violence and homophobia in lyrics (Adams & Fuller, 2006; Conrad et al., 2009; Cundiff, 2013; Damien, 2006; Monk-Turner & Sylvertooth, 2008; Rebollo-Gil & Moras, 2012; Rose, 2008; Wester et al., 1997). These topics are predominant in commercial and mainstream rap, which is performed by artists who work with major record companies (Harkness, 2013). However, the predominant topics among popular, successful underground rappers are also misogyny and hypermasculinity but include politically charged and anti-establishment lyrics to a lesser degree (Oware, 2014, p. 61). Another study (Weitzer & Kubrin, 2009) suggested that rappers whose songs portray women negatively are influenced by three major social forces: larger gender relations, local neighbourhood conditions and the music industry. In response to corporate pressures, many rappers abandon political and social messages and focus instead on material wealth and sexual exploits in order to sell records. In other words, according to Oware (2014, p. 77), "some underground rap artists intentionally obscure the boundaries between the restricted and large-scale field of production, due to hegemonic market forces". This author concluded that the distinction between bad rap (mainstream rap) and good rap (underground rap) should not be made, nuancing Bourdieu's (1993, 1996) field of cultural production, as they are not mutually exclusive. However, the target group of rap/hip-hop listeners differs, according to Elafros (2013), with non-commercial rap music being positioned among hip-hop fans and rap music producers. Accordingly, whereas mainstream rap demands black ghettocentricity, underground rap endorses inter-raciality and multiculturalism (Rodriquez, 2006).

Other studies note that female rappers are not always against misogyny and male domination (Oware, 2009). In fact, the majority of female rapper lyrics talk of women who are self-objectified, self-exploited and use derogatory lyrics when referring to other women. The author found that these contradictory messages invalidate the empowering messages that are transmitted, instead of reproducing and defending male hegemonic notions of femininity. The fact they offered such little resistance is probably a reflection of industry norms at that time (Weitzer & Kubrin, 2009), though it would seem that resistance was stronger in the beginnings (Rose, 1994).

Some authors have focused on people's perception of rap/hip-hop as well as its influence. For instance, "hip-hop was rated lowest on showing relationships being committed, nurturing, romantic, responsible, using polite language and implicit" (Agbo-Quaye & Robertson, 2010, p. 362). These authors also pointed out that "female characters within hip-hop and rock are predominantly represented as powerless and yearning for male authority". This is in line with what Berry (1995) stated a quarter of century ago when expressing that hip-hop displays sexuality, misogynistic lyrics and apparent pornographic elements, reinforcing its image of a "morally corrupted genre". In this regard, it has been said that controversial rap music has had a negative influence on adolescent development (Tanner et al., 2009). However, young people seem to be unaware of the impact that this music has on their lives (Agbo-Quaye & Robertson, 2010). For instance, cultural images of sexual stereotypes in rap music videos can influence the sexual attitudes and behaviour of female adolescents (Peterson et al., 2007). Other negative effects from a sociological point of view refer to greater acceptance of male domination and violence (Oliver, 2006).

Finally, from the consumer perspective, specifically in relation to music genre choices, Cuadrado-García et al. (2018) found, in a survey conducted among young consumers, that rap/hip-hop was one of their favourite music genres. They also showed that having studied music made a difference in terms of genre preferences. Those with a music background preferred electronic, house, dance, jazz and classical music. On the other hand, those with no musical studies preferred rap, hip-hop and Latin pop-rock to a greater extent. Other authors have highlighted that the rap consumer profile has evolved, from black young men belonging to a low social class to middle class white young men with a university degree. This has occurred all over the world (Rodriquez, 2006; Yousman, 2003). In addition, research has shown that hip-hop serves as an avenue for interaction with black culture and a proxy for interpersonal interaction with black Americans (Jacobson, 2015; Rose, 2008). Non-black fans are perceived as cultural tourists looking for a way to understand black culture (Jacobson, 2015). In summary, rap acts as an interracial socialiser, enabling white fans to learn about the effects of racism and discrimination through this music (Sullivan, 2003).

In this context, public engagement with hip-hop, due to the appearance of gangsta rap, has shifted its consumption as a commodity, following the change that began with mass marketing to larger white audiences all over the world. Specifically, this has been achieved by elites imitating the behavioural and aesthetic patterns of poor people, setting hip-hop consumption standards and fashion trends, and inverting Veblen's theory of conspicuous consumption (Hunter, 2011). This is in line with Baudrillard's (1988) theory of object relations, which captures hip-hop's consumption trend. Thus, rap music is a product that sells as a lifestyle, being reinforced by lyrics, music videos and online fan gossip (Hunter, 2011). In Europe, rap is especially linked to male migrant descendants, being a multicultural genre (Bennet, 1999; Elafros, 2013; Green, 2013; Laidlaw, 2011; Reitsamer & Prokop, 2018). It focuses on social problems and minorities' living conditions, reinforcing values as opposed to American rap (Androutsopoulos & Scholz, 2003; Beau, 1996).

More recent studies have focused on female rap audiences. Zickerman (2013) found an increasingly large female audience who appreciate its aesthetics and music, including rhythmic flow, melodic structure and the general appeal of the artist. Lyrics do not seem to be as relevant as Sullivan (2003) found years ago, when white people did not pay attention to the words of the songs as they were more attracted to the beat of the music, particularly young women. However, some of the previous issues regarding gender and the consumption of alternative music genres, specifically rap/hip-hop, still lack empirical research and need more specific analysis.

3 Research: Objectives and Methodology

Based on the above, exploratory research was conducted to find out whether there were any gender differences regarding consumption and opinions of rap/hip-hop as a music genre. Specifically, we aimed to answer the following research questions. RQ1: rap/hip-hop concert attendance habits; RQ2: degree of knowledge of this music genre; RQ3: satisfaction and interest in rap/hip-hop; RQ4: differences in habits and attitudes according to gender; RQ5: segmentation of rap/hip-hop consumers based on knowledge, interest and satisfaction levels.

The research was conducted in the form of an online survey using a structured questionnaire divided into three sections (rap/hip-hop consumption habits, attitudes towards rap/hip-hop and classification variables). Different scales of measurement were used accordingly, with questions regarding attitudes and opinions being drawn up using five-point Likert scales. Convenience sampling was chosen to select respondents from a population made up of people between 15 and 65 years of age. The questionnaire was sent to minors after requesting and receiving authorisation from their parents. A total of 150 participants answered the questionnaire. Data collection took place in March 2019. Then, after producing a dataset, univariate and multivariate analyses (ANOVA tests, cluster analysis and cross-tabulations) were calculated to statistically process the information gathered in order to answer the aforementioned research questions. For operational and logical reasons, the results shown only relate to differences in gender. The research method is summarised in Table 1.

The sample of this survey (Table 2) was comprised of 45.3% women and 54.7% men. Most of them, 72.0%, were between 15 and 24 years of age. In terms of level of studies, half were graduates (50.0%) while 86.7% were single, and 63.3% were students.

Table 1 Research methodology

Information-Gathering Technique	Online survey administered via a structured questionnaire
Questionnaire	Three parts: concert attendance habits, appreciation and sociodemographic profile Different measurement scales
Population	People between 15 and 65 years of age
Sampling Method & Sample Size	Convenience sampling: 150 respondents
Fieldwork	March 2019
Data Analysis	Univariate and multivariate using SPSS

Source Authors' own

Table 2 Sample distribution

Gender	45.3% Women 54.7% Men
Age	28.7% (15–19) 43.3% (20–24) 11.3% (25–34) 8.0% (35–44) 8.7% (>44)
Level Of Studies	26.7% Undergraduates 50.0% Graduates 23.4% Secondary education
Personal Situation	86.7% Single 13.3% Married
Occupation	63.3% Students 25.3% Employees 6.2% Self-employed 5.3% Non-active

Source Authors' own

4 Results

In relation to concert attendance habits, specifically social ones (Table 3), respondents mainly attended rap/hip-hop music concerts with their friends (80.0%). Partners were much less considered and were selected by just 11.0% of the sample. Finally, relatives had residual importance with only 2.7% of participants choosing this option. To ascertain the role of gender in relation to this habit, a cross-tabulation analysis by chi-square was calculated. Results showed that gender influences for people attending concerts with friends were more relevant for men (86.6%) than for women (72.1%). Conversely, partners were more important as companions for women (65.4%) compared to men (25.0%).

In addition, participants in the study mostly chose social networks (82.7%) to find out about rap artists/bands and concerts, followed way behind by websites (9.3%). However, no statistically significant differences regarding gender showed up in relation to this consumption habit.

Knowledge, interest and satisfaction with this music genre were measured using five-point Likert scales. The results in Table 4 show that rap/hip-hop music concert attendees were extremely satisfied with the experience (4.39 out of 5). Interest in this music genre was also high (4.06) but knowledge of this alternative genre was lower, although greater than the midpoint of the scale (3.51). ANOVA tests show that men and women only had a significantly different knowledge of this music genre, with men scoring higher than women, 3.66 and 3.32, respectively.

Participants were grouped using a double cluster analysis: hierarchical and non-hierarchical. By interpreting the resulting dendrogram, the first method showed that three was the optimal solution. The non-hierarchical k-means method helped to describe these three clusters, as summarised in Table 5. Cluster 1 was comprised of individuals' satisfaction, knowledge and interest in rap to a greater extent. In

Table 3 Social attendance habits in rap/hip-hop by gender

I go with	Total %	Men %	Women %
Friends	80.0	86.6	72.1
Partner	11.0	25.0	65.4
Relatives	2.7	2.4	2.9

Chi-Square Test Sig. (0.072)
Source Authors' own

Table 4 Knowledge, interest and satisfaction

Items	Min	Max	Total	Std. D	Men	Women	Sig. (ANOVA)
Knowledge	1	5	3.51	1.060	3.66	3.32	0.054*
Interest	1	5	4.06	1.018	4.12	3.99	0.415
Satisfaction	1	5	4.39	0.933	4.34	4.44	0.516

Source Authors' own

Table 5 Clusters

Clusters	Knowledge	Interest	Satisfaction	Sig	Number
1: Involved	4	4	5	0.000	78
2: Apathetic	2	2	3	0.000	20
3: Hedonists	3	3	5	0.000	52

Source Authors' own

cluster 2, the three previous variables obtained the lowest scores. Finally, those in cluster 3 valued satisfaction highly but not the other variables. As a result, clusters were respectively labelled: involved (cluster 1), apathetic (cluster 2) and hedonists (cluster 3).

Although there were no significative differences between groups according to gender, women were more numerous in cluster 2. Significant differences arose when the variable belonging to a cluster with sociodemographic variables such as age (Sig. 0.001), level of studies (Sig. 0.000), marital status (Sig. 0.000) and occupation was cross-tabulated. In this sense, those in cluster 1 were the youngest while cluster 2 members were older. In addition, in segment 1, the percentages of respondents with primary, secondary and bachelor studies were higher, while the percentage of respondents with university studies was similar in clusters 1 and 3. Regarding marital status, there were more single and married people in cluster 1, while divorced people were the majority in segment 2. The percentage of students was higher in cluster 3 while in cluster 2 the percentage of employees was higher.

Similarly, differences were also found when cross-tabulating cluster membership and behavioural variables, specifically, the frequency of attendance at rap music concerts (Sig. 0.000) and the last time people attended a concert (Sig. 0.001). Individuals in cluster 1 were frequent attendees, obtaining higher percentages in almost all the options except once a year, which was slightly higher for those in cluster 3. Likewise, cluster 1 members scored higher in attending rap concerts more recently than the other two groups, followed by those in cluster 3. All these traits confirmed the labels assigned to the three clusters based on their relationship with knowledge, interest and satisfaction with rap/hip-hop.

5 Discussion

Music consumption has been studied in different academic disciplines, such as psychology, sociology, economics and marketing. These disciplines have dealt both directly and indirectly with the issues of gender and alternative music genres, specifically rap/hip-hop participation. In doing so, literature has shown major differences in relation to music preferences, social identity, social demographics, perceptions, cultural capital and consumption patterns. An exploratory survey was conducted to obtain a deeper insight into rap/hip-hop consumption by gender, trying to overcome a certain gap in the literature. Specifically, the aim was to analyse rap music consumption habits and how they were evaluated as well as to segment participants based on satisfaction, interest and knowledge about rap/hip-hop.

Results show that rap is a minority music genre whose main audience is single men under 24, who are mainly students taking upper secondary or graduate studies. However, the increasing participation of women in this music genre is worth noting. These findings corroborate previous studies. Specifically, Rodriquez (2006) pointed out that young men were predominant in rap consumption independently of their race. Likewise, the results confirm that rap has become part of global popular culture (Laidlaw, 2011). The findings are also in line with Herrera et al. (2018) who declared a greater male preference towards styles considered to be "hard", such as rap. The increasing participation of women also coincides with the findings indicated by Langmeyer et al. (2012) who stated that men were more mutually exclusive in their music preferences, while women allowed a greater overlap.

In addition, gender influences some social attendance habits in relation to rap/hip-hop music concerts. In this regard, men attend this sort of cultural events mostly with friends, reinforcing their identity as a group. Conversely, women usually go to rap concerts with their partners. This could be indicative of an indirect interest in this music genre. These results confirm Tipa's (2015) statement that the use of music by men plays a major role in social and affective relationships established between peer groups. Similarly, North (2010) pointed out that while men listen to music in the search for social membership with their peer group, women listen to music as a way to satisfy their emotional needs and for moments of pleasure.

The existence of high levels of knowledge, interest and satisfaction among consumers of this music genre is also noteworthy, being greater in men, though significant differences only arose between men and women in terms of rap knowledge. This enables us to state that there could be a reduction in the gender gap in rap/hip-hop consumption. This can also be confirmed by the existence of three segments after conducting a double cluster analysis, in which gender did not lead to significant differences. In other words, the involved, apathetic and hedonist segments were made up of both men and women.

In parallel, according to secondary data, digital technologies, such as social networks and music platforms, have also played an important role in rap/hip-hop consumption and have contributed to closing the gender gap. These technologies have fostered greater production, better accessibility, higher visibility and enhanced knowledge as well as broader music audiences, as shown in the study by Simoes and Campos (2017). This is the case of women increasingly consuming both live and recorded rap music in spite of their mostly controversial lyrics. Not paying attention to the words of rap songs and being more attracted to the rhythm of the music, as pointed out by Sullivan (2003), or being unaware of the impact of this music in their lives (Agbo-Quaye & Robertson, 2010) could explain this phenomenon. To sum up, the increasing female rap/hip-hop audience seems to be based on its appreciation of its aesthetics and music, rhythmic flow, melodic structure and the appeal of the artist, as Zickerman (2013) confirmed.

This research, although novel in its aim and offering relevant results in terms of live rap consumption and gender, has certain limitations. Its exploratory nature and the non-probability sampling method selected to choose a limited sample make it difficult to generalise the results. Finally, not having used more precise measurement scales hinders a more accurate interpretation of results. However, the study could be duplicated via a new line of research.

Acknowledgements Authors wish to thank María Quílez for her help in the research design and fieldwork.

References

Adams, T. M., & Fuller, D. B. (2006). The words have changed but the ideology remains the same: Misogynistic lyrics in rap music. *Journal of Black Studies, 36*(6), 938–957. https://doi.org/10.1177%2F0021934704274072.
Agbo-Quaye, S., & Robertson, T. (2010). The motorway to adulthood: Music preference as the sex and relationships roadmap. *Sex Education, 10*(4), 359–371. https://doi.org/10.1080/14681811.2010.515094.
Androutsopoulos, J. K., & Scholz, A. (2003). Spaghetti Funk: Appropriations of hip-hop culture and rap music in Europe. *Popular Music and Society, 26*(4), 463–479. https://doi.org/10.1080/0300776032000144922.
Allen, R. L. (2001). *The concept of self: A study of black identity and self-esteem.* Wayne State University Press.
Appiah, O. (2004). Effects of ethnic identification on web browsers' attitudes toward and navigational patterns on race-targeted sites. *Communication Research, 31*(3), 312–337. https://doi.org/10.1177%2F0093650203261515.
Baudrillard, J. (1988). The system of objects. In M. Poster, *Jean Baudrillard: Selected Writings* (pp. 3–31). Stanford University Press.
Beau, A. (1996). Hip hop and rap in Europe: The culture of the urban ghetto's. In P. Rutten (Ed.), *Music, culture and society in Europe* (pp. 129–134). European Music Office.
Bennett, A. (1999). Hip hop am Main: The localization of rap music and hip-hop culture. *Media Culture and Society, 21*(1), 77–91. https://doi.org/10.1177%2F016344399021001004.
Berry, V. (1995). Redeeming the rap music experience. In J. S Epstein, *Adolescents and their music: If it's too loud, you're too old* (Vol. 1, pp. 165–87). Garland Publishing.
Bihagen, E., & Katz-Gerro, T. (2000). Culture participation in Sweden: The stability of gender differences. *Poetics, 27*(5–6), 327–349. https://doi.org/10.1016/S0304-422X(00)00004-8.
Bonneville-Roussy, A., Rentfrow, P. J., Xu, M. K., & Potter, J. (2013). Music through the ages: Trends in musical engagement and preferences from adolescence through middle adulthood. *Journal of Personality and Social Psychology, 105*(4), 703–717. https://doi.org/10.1037/a0033770.
Bourdieu, P. (1984). *Distinction: A social critique on the judgment of taste.* Harvard University Press.
Bourdieu, P. (1993). *The field of cultural production.* Columbia University Press.
Bourdieu, P. (1996). *The rules of art: Genesis and structure of the literary field.* Stanford University Press.
Christin, A. (2012). Gender and highbrow cultural participation in the United States. *Poetics, 40*(5), 423–443. https://doi.org/10.1016/j.poetic.2012.07.003.

Colley, A. (2008). Young people's musical taste: Relationship with gender and gender-related traits. *Journal of Applied Social Psychology, 38*(8), 2039–2055. https://doi.org/10.1111/j.1559-1816.2008.00379.x.

Collins, R. (1988). Women and men in the class structure. *Journal of Family Issues, 9*(1), 27–50. https://doi.org/10.1177%2F019251388009001003.

Conrad, K., Dixon, L., & Zhang, Y. (2009). Controversial rap themes, gender portrayals and skin tone distortion: A content analysis of rap music videos. *Journal of Broadcasting and Electronic Media, 53*(1), 134–156. https://doi.org/10.1080/08838150802643795.

Crowther, R., & Durkin, K. (1982). Sex- and age-related differences in the musical behaviour, interest, and attitudes towards music of 232 secondary school students. *Education Studies, 8*(2), 131–139. https://doi.org/10.1080/0305569820080206.

Cuadrado-García, M., Montoro-Pons, J. D., & González-Casal, P. (2018). *Spontaneous versus suggested recall of music genres preference. An exploratory research with young people.* ACEI 2018 International Conference, Melbourne, Australia.

Cundiff, G. (2013). The Influence of rap/hip hop music: A mixed method analysis on audience perceptions and misogynistic lyrics and the issue of domestic violence. *The Elon Journal of Undergraduate Research in Communications, 4*(11), 71–82. http://www.inquiriesjournal.com/a?id=792..

Damien, A. (2006). Hip hop consumption and masculinity. In L. Stevens & J. Borgerson (Eds.), *GCB—Gender and Consumer Behavior* (Vol. 8, pp. 104–116). Association for Consumer Research.

Delsing, M. J., Ter Bogt, T. F., Engels, R. C., & Meeus, W. H. (2008). Adolescents' music preferences and personality characteristics. *European Journal of Personality, 22*(2), 109–130. https://doi.org/10.1002/per.665.

DiMaggio, P. (1982). Cultural capital and school success: The impact of status culture participation on the grades of U.S. High School students. *American Sociological Review, 47*(2), 189–210. https://doi.org/10.2307/2094962.

Dixon, T., Zhang, Y., & Conrad, K. (2009). Self-esteem, misogyny and Afrocentricity: An examination of the relationship between rap music consumption and African-American perceptions. *Group Process Intergroup Relationship, 12*(3), 345–360. https://doi.org/10.1177%2F1368430209102847.

Elafros, A. (2013). Greek hip hop: Local and translocal authentication in the restricted field of production. *Poetics, 41*(1), 75–95. https://doi.org/10.1016/j.poetic.2012.11.002.

Eysenck, H. J. (1990). Biological dimensions of personality. In L. A. Pervin (Ed.), *Handbook of Personality: Theory and Research* (pp. 244–276). Guilford Press.

Favaro, D., & Frateschi, P. (2007). A Discrete choice model of consumption of cultural goods. The case of music. *Journal of Cultural Economics, 31*, 205–231. https://doi.org/10.1007/s10824-007-9043-x.

García-Álvarez, E., Katz-Gerro, T., & López-Sintas, J. (2007). Deconstructing cultural omnivorousness 1982–2002: Heterology in Americans' musical preferences. *Social Forces, 86*(2), 417–443. https://doi.org/10.1093/sf/86.2.417.

George, D., Stickle, K., Rachid, F., & Wopnford, A. (2007). The association between types of music enjoyed and cognitive, behavioral, and personality factors of those who listen. *Psychomusicology A Journal of Research in Music Cognition, 19*(2), 32–56. https://doi.org/10.1037/h0094035.

Green, S. (2013). The musical routes of the Spanish Black Atlantic: The performance of identities in the rap of Frank T and El Chojín. *Popular Music and Society, 36*(4), 505–522. https://doi.org/10.1080/03007766.2012.681112.

Harkness, G. (2013). Gangs and gangsta rap in Chicago: A microscenes perspective. *Poetics, 41*(2), 151–176. https://doi.org/10.1016/j.poetic.2013.01.001.

Herrera, L., Soares-Quadros, J. F., Jr., & Lorenzo, O. (2018). Music preferences and personality in Brazilians. *Frontier in Psychology, 9*(1488), 1–12. https://doi.org/10.3389/fpsyg.2018.01488.

Hunter, M. (2011). Shake it, baby, shake it: Consumption and the new gender relation in hip-hop. *Sociological Perspectives, 54*(1), 15–36. https://doi.org/10.1525%2Fsop.2011.54.1.15.

Jacobson, G. (2015). Racial formation theory and systemic racism in Hip Hop fans' perceptions. *Sociological Forum, 30*(3), 832–851. https://doi.org/10.1111/socf.12186.

Katz-Gerro, T., & Osullivan, O. (2010). Voracious cultural consumption intertwining of gender with social status. *Time and Society, 19*(2), 193–219. https://doi.org/10.1177%2F0961463X09 354422.

Laidlaw, A. (2011). *Blackness in the absence of blackness: White appropriations of rap music and hip-hop Culture in Newcastle upon Tyne—Explaining a cultural shift*. Loughborough University. U.K Thesis. https://hdl.handle.net/2134/8389.

Langmeyer, A., Guglhör-Rudan, A., & Tarnai, C. (2012). What do music preferences reveal about personality? *Journal of Individual Differences, 33*(2), 119–130. https://doi.org/10.1027/1614-0001/a000082.

Lizardo, O. (2004). The cognitive origins of Bourdieu's habitus. *Journal for the Theory of Social Behavior, 34*(4), 375–401. https://doi.org/10.1111/j.1468-5914.2004.00255.x.

Lizardo, O. (2006). The puzzle of women's "highbrow" culture consumption: Integrating gender and work into Bourdieu's class theory of taste. *Poetics, 34*(1), 1–23. https://doi.org/10.1016/j.poetic.2005.09.001.

McNamara, L., & Ballard, M. E. (1999). Resting arousal, sensation seeking, and music preference. *Genetic, Social, and General Psychology Monographs, 125*(3), 229–250. https://search.proquest.com/docview/231470962?accountid=14744.

Ministerio de Cultura y Deportes. (2019). *Encuesta de Hábitos y Prácticas Culturales 2018–2019*. http://www.culturaydeporte.gob.es/dam/jcr:1712f192-d59b-427d-bbe0-db0f3e9f716b/encuesta-de-habitos-y-practicas-culturales-2018-2019.pdf.

Monk-Turner, E., & Sylvertooth, D. (2008). Rap music: Gender difference in derogatory word use. *American Communication Journal, 10*(4), 1–12. https://digitalcommons.odu.edu/sociology_criminaljustice_fac_pubs/19.

Montoro-Pons, J. D., & Cuadrado-García, M. (2011). Live and prerecorded popular music consumption. *Journal of Cultural Economics, 35*(1), 19–48. https://doi.org/10.1007/s10824-010-9130-2.

North, A. (2010). Individual differences in musical taste. *American Journal of Psychology*, 123(2), 199–208. https://doi.org/10.5406/amerjpsyc.123.2.0199.

Oliver, W. (2006). "The Street" an alternative black male socialization institution. *Journal of Black Studies, 36*(6), 918–937. https://doi.org/10.1177%2F0021934704273445.

Oware, M. (2009). A "man's woman"? contradictory messages in the songs of female rappers, 1992–2000. *Journal of Black Studies, 39*(5),786–802. https://doi.org/10.1177%2F0021934707 302454.

Oware, M. (2014). (Un) conscious (popular) underground: Restricted cultural production and underground rap music. *Poetics, 42*, 60–81. https://doi.org/10.1016/j.poetic.2013.12.001.

Peterson, R. A. (1992). Understanding audience segmentation: From elites and mass omnivore and univore. *Poetics, 21*(4), 243–258. https://doi.org/10.1016/0304-422X(92)90008-Q.

Peterson, R. A., & Kern, R. (1996). Changing highbrow taste: From snob to omnivore. *American Sociological Review, 61*(5), 900–907. https://doi.org/10.2307/2096460.

Peterson, S., Wingood, G., DiClemente, R., Harrington, K., & Davies, D. (2007). Images of sexual stereotypes in rap videos and the health of African American female adolescents. *Journal of Women's Health, 16*(8), 1157–1164. https://doi.org/10.1089/jwh.2007.0429.

Prieto-Rodríguez, J., & Fernández Blanco, V. (2000). Are popular and classical music listeners the same people? *Journal of Cultural Economics, 24*, 147–216. https://doi.org/10.1023/A:100762 0605785.

Rebollo-Gil, G., & Moras, A. (2012). Black women and black men in hip hop music: Misogyny, violence and the negotiation of (white-owned) space. *The Journal of Popular Culture, 45*(1), 118–132. https://doi.org/10.1111/j.1540-5931.2011.00898.x.

Reitsamer, R., & Prokop, R. (2018). Keepin' it real in Central Europe: The DIY rap music careers of male hip hop artists in Austria. *Cultural Sociology, 12*(2), 193–207. https://doi.org/10.1177% 2F1749975517694299.

Rentfrow, P. J., & Gosling, S. D. (2003). The do re mi's of everyday life: The structure and personality correlates of music preferences. *Journal of Personality and Social Psychology, 84*(6), 1236–1256. https://psycnet.apa.org/doi/10.1037/0022-3514.84.6.1236.

Rentfrow, P. J., & Gosling, S. D. (2006). Message in a ballad. The role of music preferences in interpersonal perception. *Psychological Science, 17*(39), 236–242. https://doi.org/10.1111%2Fj.1467-9280.2006.01691.x.

Rentfrow, P. J., & Gosling, S. D. (2007). The content and validity of music-genre stereotypes among college students. *Psychology of Music, 35*(2), 306–326. https://doi.org/10.1177%2F0305735607070382.

Rentfrow, P. J., Goldberg, L. R., & Levitin, D. J. (2011). The structure of musical preferences: A Five-Factor Model. *Journal of Personality and Social Psychology, 100*(6): 1139–1157. https://psycnet.apa.org/doi/10.1037/a0022406.

Rentfrow, P. J., Goldberg, L. R., Stillwell, D. J., Kosinski, M., & Levitin, D. J. (2012). The song remains the same: A replication and extension of the MUSIC Model. *Music Perception, 30*(2), 161–185. https://doi.org/10.1525/mp.2012.30.2.161.

Rodriquez, J. (2006). Color-blind ideology and the cultural appropriation of hip-hop. *Journal of Contemporary Ethnography, 35*(6), 645–668. https://doi.org/10.1177%2F0891241606286997.

Rose, T. (1994). *Black noise: Rap Music and Black Culture in Contemporary America.* Wesleyan University Press.

Rose, T. (2008). *The hip hop wars: What we talk about when we talk about hip hop and Why it matters.* Basic Civitas Books.

Rosengren, K. E., Wenner, L. A., & Palmgreen, P. (1985). *Media gratifications research.* Sage.

Schäfer, T., & Sedlmeier, P. (2010). What makes us like music? Determinants of music preference. *Psychology of Aesthetics, Creativity and the Arts, 4*(4), 223–234. https://doi.org/10.1037/a0018374.

Simoes, J. A., & Campos, R. (2017). Digital media, subcultural activity and youth participation: The cases of protest rap and graffiti in Portugal. *Journal of Youth Studies, 20*(1), 16–31. https://doi.org/10.1080/13676261.2016.1166190.

Sullivan, R. (2003). Rap and race: It's got a nice beat, but what about the message? *Journal of Black Studies, 33*(5), 605–622. https://doi.org/10.1177%2F0021934703033005004.

Tanner, J., Asbridge, M., & Wortley, S. (2009). Listening to rap: Cultures of crime, cultures of resistance. *Social Forces, 88*(2), 693–722. https://doi.org/10.1353/sof.0.0271.

Tipa, J. (2015). Una aproximación a clase social, género y etnicidad en el consumo de música entre los estudiantes de la Universidad Intercultural de Chiapas [An approach to social class, gender and ethnicity in the music consumption among the students of the Intercultural University of Chiapas]. *Cuicuilco, 22*, 91–112.

Weitzer, R., & Kubrin, C. (2009). Misogyny in rap music: A content analysis of prevalence and meanings. *Men and Masculinities, 12*(1), 3–29. https://doi.org/10.1177%2F1097184X08327696.

Wester, S. R., Crown, C. L., Quotan, G. L., & Heesacker, M. (1997). The influence of sexually violent rap music on attitude of men with little prior exposure. *Psychology of Women Quarterly, 21*(4), 497–508. https://doi.org/10.1111/j.1471-6402.1997.tb00127.x.

Yousman, B. (2003). Blackophilia and blackophobia: White youth, the consumption of rap music, and white supremacy. *Communication Theory, 13*(4), 366–391. https://doi.org/10.1111/j.1468-2885.2003.tb00297.x.

Zickerman, S. C. (2013). *The effects of hip hop and rap on young women in Academia* (Thesis, University of Toronto, Canada). http://hdl.handle.net/1807/36081.

Zweigenhaft, R. L. (2008). A do re mi encore: A closer look at the personality correlates of music preferences. *Journal of Individual Differences, 29*, 45–55. https://doi.org/10.1027/1614-0001.29.1.45.

Zuckerman, M. (1979). *Sensation seeking: Beyond the optimal level of arousal.* Erlbaum.

Open Access This chapter is licensed under the terms of the Creative Commons Attribution 4.0 International License (http://creativecommons.org/licenses/by/4.0/), which permits use, sharing, adaptation, distribution and reproduction in any medium or format, as long as you give appropriate credit to the original author(s) and the source, provide a link to the Creative Commons license and indicate if changes were made.

The images or other third party material in this chapter are included in the chapter's Creative Commons license, unless indicated otherwise in a credit line to the material. If material is not included in the chapter's Creative Commons license and your intended use is not permitted by statutory regulation or exceeds the permitted use, you will need to obtain permission directly from the copyright holder.

Music and Territory: The Case of Bands in the Valencian Region

The Intangible Cultural Landscape of the Banda Primitiva de Llíria

Virginia Santamarina-Campos⊙, José Luis Gasent-Blesa⊙, Pau Alcocer-Torres, and Mª Ángeles Carabal-Montagud⊙

1 Introduction: Popular Music Tradition as Intangible and Creative Cultural Heritage

The first references to ethnographic and ethnological heritage in the general norms of cultural heritage in Spain appear in Spanish Royal Decree-Law, dated 9 August 1926, which mentions its typical and picturesque character, and in the Spanish Law on the Defence, Conservation and Enhancement of National Historical-artistic Heritage, of 13 May 1933, which refers to picturesque places that must be preserved. It is not until the Spanish decrees of 1953 and 1961 that the term "ethnological" is used for the first time in terms of cultural heritage, providing an initial approach to the concept of intangible heritage related to the traditional and popular and associating it with folklore. Yet it was not until the 1978 Spanish Constitution that a conceptual framework was provided for intangible heritage, which proved to be a pioneering concept in the European constitutional context.

In the 1985 Spanish Historical Heritage Law, an important advance was perceived in the definition of ethnographic and ethnological heritage, taking in current phenomena and considering other types of goods that do not have to be material, and although there continues to be a relationship between the "ethnological" and the "traditional", traditional culture does not have to refer to the past.

In 1989, for the first time, the UNESCO mentioned intangible and intangible assets in the Recommendation on the Safeguarding of Traditional and Popular Culture

---

V. Santamarina-Campos (✉) · M. Á. Carabal-Montagud
Universitat Politècnica de València, Valencia, Spain
e-mail: virsanca@upv.es

J. L. Gasent-Blesa
Universitat de València, Valencia, Spain

P. Alcocer-Torres
Colegio Helios, Valencia, Spain

© The Author(s) 2021
B. de-Miguel-Molina et al. (eds.), *Music as Intangible Cultural Heritage*, SpringerBriefs in Economics,
https://doi.org/10.1007/978-3-030-76882-9_6

(UNESCO, 1989), moving towards the recognition of other forms and categories of heritage, indicating that "Traditional and popular is part of the universal heritage of humanity and is a powerful means of rapprochement between existing peoples and social groups and the affirmation of their cultural identity" (UNESCO, 1989). In addition, the Recommendation defined traditional and popular culture as the "set of creations that emanate from a cultural community based on tradition, expressed by a group or by individuals, and that recognise that they respond to the expectations of the community regarding the expression of their cultural and social identity; norms and values are transmitted orally, by imitation or in other ways. Its forms include, among others, language, literature, music, dance, games, mythology, rites, customs, crafts, architecture and other arts" (UNESCO, 1989).

It was not until 1997 when a further step was taken in the International Consultation on the Preservation of Popular Cultural Spaces (UNESCO, 1998), organised in Marrakech by the Division of Cultural Heritage and the Moroccan National Commission for UNESCO, in which the distinction of Oral and Intangible Heritage was made as the heritage of humanity. Despite this progress, in the new additions to the list of world heritage sites, the materialistic and monumental vision has continued to prevail, with non-material heritage forms being relegated. In 2001, for the first time, 19 spaces and relevant forms of expression were declared Masterpieces of the Oral and Intangible Heritage of Humanity (UNESCO, 2001). The programme concluded in 2006 with the entry into force of the Convention for the Safeguarding of the Intangible Cultural Heritage (UNESCO, 2003), which was ratified in Spain in 2007, becoming part of its internal legal system. Thus, in 2008, the new Representative List of the Intangible Cultural Heritage of Humanity (UNESCO, 2008) was created, bringing together the 90 elements declared masterpieces of oral and intangible heritage in 2001, 2003 and 2005.

Spanish legislation accompanied the advances made at international level in the National Plan for the Safeguarding of Intangible Cultural Heritage, which was approved in 2011 (Ministerio de Cultura y Deporte, 2011) and in Law 10/2015, of 26 May 2015, for the Safeguarding of Intangible Cultural Heritage. In the case of the Valencian Region, its exclusive powers in terms of Valencian Cultural Heritage were implemented via Valencian Regional Government Law 4/1998, of 11 June, on Valencian Cultural Heritage (Generalitat Valenciana, 1998), which established the inclusion of ethnological heritage's intangible assets as an instrument for the protection of intangible cultural heritage, the values of which must be specially preserved and known, in the General Inventory of Valencian Cultural Heritage.

In this framework, Valencian popular musical tradition materialised by musical societies (Bands in the Valencian Region) was declared as an Intangible Asset of Local Relevance in 2011 and was included in the General Inventory of Valencian Cultural Heritage (Generalitat Valenciana, 2011). Later, in May 2018, the popular musical tradition of the Valencian Region was declared as an Asset of Intangible Cultural Interest (Generalitat Valenciana, 2018). This brought the Banda Primitiva de Llíria under the protection and safeguarding umbrella that is specified in the following measures (Generalitat Valenciana, 2018):

(a) To carry out identification, description, research, study and documentation tasks with scientific criteria.
(b) To incorporate the available testimonies into material supports that guarantee their protection and preservation.
(c) To ensure the normal development and survival of this cultural manifestation, as well as to protect the conservation of its traditional values and their transmission to future generations.

In addition, recently, the musical societies of the Valencian Community have been declared a Representative Manifestation of the Intangible Cultural Heritage in Spain, recognising the patrimonial value of the movement of the musical societies that make up the Valencian Community (FSMCV 2021a).

On the other hand, it is important to note that, in 2019, Llíria was declared as a UNESCO City of Music under the broader Creative Cities Network (UNESCO, 2019), recognising a long musical history that dates back to the third century BC, and confirming that music constitutes a fundamental part of the town's cultural identity. The UNESCO Creative Cities Network was created in 2004 with the aim of promoting cooperation between cities that identify creativity as a strategic factor for sustainable urban development. Currently, the 246 cities that make up the Network work together with the aim of positioning creativity and cultural industries at the centre of their local development plans (UNESCO, 2020).

2 Methodological Approach

A qualitative research method was used to develop the work mainly focusing on documentary and field research. The study of documentary sources included the analysis of bibliographic sources, and especially archive research, mainly the Banda Primitiva de Llíria's Archive, the *Ateneo Musical y de Enseñanza Banda Primitiva de Llíria* (Music and Teaching Athenaeum of the Banda Primitiva de Llíria), and the Miguel Blat Ibáñez Collection at the Valencian Institute of Culture (IVC) of the Valencian Regional Government. On the other hand, the fieldwork focused on the use of tools such as participant observation and semi-guided interviews.

3 Challenges of the Popular Music Tradition in Llíria

In the specific case of the Valencian Region, the musical phenomenon of bands has been a key part of the associative framework of the territory (Asensi Silvestre, 2008). The Valencian Region enjoys a long musical tradition which, through its municipal bands and music schools, trains over 60,000 students, giving rise to 1,100 bands, which bring together around 40,000 musicians in 500 musical societies, representing half of those existing in Spain (Cultural València, 2018; SGAE, 2020). These bands play a fundamental role in supporting most of the traditions and popular festivals in the Valencian Region, in which musical works or songs which are not their own are used, such as the pasodobles in the Fallas festival in Valencia, or in works that are created especially, as is the case of the compositions for the Moors and Christians festivals, which annually premiere pasodobles and Moorish and Christian marches (Bottle Nicolás, 2019). In addition, it should be noted that bands are present in 95% of the municipalities with more than 500 inhabitants, contributing around €40 million to regional GDP (Cultural València, 2018). The crisis derived from COVID-19 has significantly affected the Valencian Region's musical societies, which suffered estimated economic losses of about €20 million in 2020 (SGAE, 2020). From a social point of view, the pandemic has constituted a framework to reaffirm and reinforce the importance of the social function of bands, which was showcased in the #WindowsOfMusicAndHope campaign on social networks, which aimed to spread a message of hope and at the same time to raise awareness about the importance of staying at home. In this new uncertain environment, music has been a way to unite people and help them overcome the difficulties they face due to social distancing measures (UNESCO, 2019), once again demonstrating its ability to mobilise and encourage new recruits, even in new cultural environments such as social networks.

The choice of the town of Llíria is justified because of its strong musical society culture which has been in existence since the nineteenth century. At that time, this civic band phenomenon was represented in the town by the musical groups of Música Vella (old music) or Primitiva and Música Nova (new music), the latter formed in the middle of the nineteenth century by a split from the Música Vella, but which disappeared at the end of the nineteenth century (Martín Montañés, 1994). At the beginning of the twentieth century, rivalry began between the Banda Primitiva and the new ensemble Unió Musical, serving as a vehicle for cultural transmission and at the same time configuring a fragmented local identity due to the artistic rivalry between the two (Asensi Silvestre, 2008).

The history of Llíria has been linked to tradition and band rivalry since the nineteenth century, and the town cannot currently be understood without them, as Llíria would be completely different (Informant 2). The existing musical rivalry in Llíria is also evident in the urban framework itself, where a street and commemorative plaques mark the division between the two areas of the bands, delimiting cultural and religious spaces. Thus, the Raval neighbourhood and the church of St Francis of Assisi are reserved for the Banda Primitiva, and the old town next to the church of Our Lady of Remedies is for the Unió Musical band (Informant 2).

On the other hand, in the specific case of the Banda Primitiva de Llíria, the musical society culture has reinforced the deeply rooted ideas and feelings of identity among the town's inhabitants that are part of this culture, to the point of linking their demonym with their belonging to said band (Informant 2).

For these reasons and following the guidelines of the Convention for the Safeguarding of Intangible Cultural Heritage (UNESCO, 2003), this work aims to support the safeguarding, respect and awareness at local, national and international level of the Banda Primitiva de Llíria, and the enhancement of one of the oldest civic bands in Spain (Banda Primitiva de Llíria, 2009a), with the aim of encouraging local, national and international dialogue centred on promoting cooperation between musical societies. The objective is to provide greater visibility and create positive recognition of the fundamental importance of this form of heritage for social cohesion and development, in an environment that has been transformed into one of collective action, solidarity, shared culture and creativity (Rausell Köster, 2013).

It is remarkable that the term civic band includes the amateur band (also known as community band) and the professional band (Rodríguez Lorenzo, 2014).

4 Historical Contextualisation of Llíria

Llíria is located in the northwest of the province of Valencia and is 25 km from the city of Valencia. It is the capital of the Camp de Turia area. Its municipal district has an extension of 229.82 km^2 and is one of the largest in the Valencian Region. It has a contrasting landscape between a mountainous area which marks the start of the Sierra Calderona and an orchard area on the left bank of the River Turia (Ayuntamiento de Llíria, 2020a). In the last official population census published by the National Institute of Statistics, Llíria had a population of 23,482 inhabitants (INE, 2020).

Llíria is a city with an extensive cultural heritage. On the one hand, it has a long musical tradition, playing host to musical societies whose musicians and board members receive no financial compensation for their work. These societies are the Banda Primitiva, the Unió Musical, the Orquesta de Plectro "*El Micalet*", the Agrupación Musical Edetana "Vicente Giménez" and the Banda Musical Unión Democrática de Pensionistas (Ayuntamiento de Llíria, 2019). Both the Banda Primitiva and the Unió Musical are famous for the numerous domestic and international awards they have received (Ayuntamiento de Llíria, 2020b). In addition, the town houses one of the most significant archaeological and monumental complexes in the entire Valencian Region (Ayuntamiento de Llíria, 2020b). The oldest remains in the municipality of Llíria date back to the late Upper Paleolithic. In the Eneolithic period, there was an important town on the edge of the Rambla Castellarda (Bonet Rosado et al., 2014), which seems to have lasted until the early Bronze Age. Remains from this age have been found in the Torreta and the Cova del Cavall (Donat Zopo & Gascó Martínez, 1973), and several settlements in Castillarejo de Peñarroya, in Lloma del Camí del Cavall, in Tossal de San Miguel (Saint Michael's Hill) and in Cova Foradà, all of which were occupied later during the Iberian period and even during Roman rule. The last two periods are especially important, and the town has been declared a Site of Cultural Interest.

As already mentioned, the current city of Llíria has its roots in the Bronze Age, in the establishment there was on the Saint Michael's Hill towards the middle of the second millennium BC (Hermosilla Pla, 2011e). This was continued in the Iberian town of Edeta, which was the capital of Edetania. Two other Iberian villages are also located in the municipality of Llíria: La Monravana and El Castellet de Bernabé (Rosado et al., 2008). Its political and economic importance, as well as its strategic position, led it to play an important role in the Roman civil wars. In Roman times, because of its desire to remain faithful to the Republican faction, it was destroyed by Sertorio's troops in 76 BC, which is why its inhabitants moved to the plain and built a new city with entirely Roman features (Pla de l'Arc settlement). The city of Edeta-Lauro was of paramount importance during the first and second centuries, while the decline that began in the third century and was accentuated in subsequent centuries could have been a parallel consequence of the growth of Valentia (today Valencia) (Hermosilla Pla, 2011e). It is important to highlight that in the Iberian culture, Edeta, as the town was known during that period, already had a strong link with music, as reflected in the ceramics of Saint Michael's Hill, with some of the best known representing Iberian images of individuals playing musical instruments (Cardiel, 2017).

During the Visigothic period, the Roman baths of Mura (Tormo-Esteve, 2018) were reused as a Christian monastery, although during the seventh century the Pla de l'Arc settlement, where the baths were located, was completely abandoned. In the Muslim period, the town was the residential headquarters of the Qadi, a kind of Muslim judge or magistrate appointed directly by the caliph.

In the year 1090, El Cid besieged the city, but left the site without taking it after the Queen Constanza, wife of Alfonso VI, required his help to fight the Almoravids in Andalusia (Hermosilla Pla, 2011c).

James I of Aragon took the city that lived under Muslim rule in 1238 and gave it to the Infante Fernando. Although Llíria was always a royal town, it had several manors such as that of María Fernández in 1293 and of the Infante Juan from 1337. The expulsion of the Moriscos in 1609 did not dramatically affect the town since it had a population of old Christians mostly (Hermosilla Pla, 2011d).

In 1707, King Felipe V created the Duchy of Llíria to reward the services of the Duke of Berwick, who was victorious in the Battle of Almansa (War of Succession), and granted it to him. The first duke, James Fitz-James Stuart, was the son of James II, King of England. He was Marshal of France and Captain General of Spain during the War of Succession. The third Duke of Llíria, Jacobo Felipe Fitz-James Stuart y Silva, married María Teresa de Silva y Haro, Duchess of Alba. From this moment on, the title of Duke of Llíria passed into the hands of the House of Alba (Hermosilla Pla, 2011d).

During the eighteenth century, the physiocratic policy of the Bourbons gave rise to spectacular advances in the agriculture in the town. In later times, during the War of Independence, the population abandoned the urban area and took refuge in the mountains. The French troops occupied the town from 1810 to 1813 and made forts in the sanctuary of Saint Michael (Saint Michael's Hill). Llíria was sacked during the Civil War of 1836 by the Carlist troops of General Cabrera on numerous occasions. In 1887, by royal decree, Llíria was granted the title of city. It should be remembered that the historical events of the time are fundamental to understand the development of the Banda Primitiva, since it is closely linked to the events that took place in the turbulent nineteenth century. An example of this is the obvious connection between the Napoleonic occupation and the process of ecclesiastical confiscation in the creation of the Banda Primitiva (Hermosilla Pla, 2011a).

5 Origin of the Banda Primitiva de Llíria

The Ateneo Musical y de Enseñanza Banda Primitiva de Llíria has its headquarters in Llíria, located in the historic Raval neighbourhood, in the northwest of the town. The origins of this musical society date back to 1819, a date that is taken as a reference and the reason for celebrating its 200th anniversary in 2019. This date has been mentioned by authors such as Domingo Uriel (Uriel, 1946), Salvador Seguí (in Badenes Masó, 1992), Roberto Martín Montañés (Martín Montañés, 1994), Vicente Galbís (in Casares Rodicio, 2006) and Juan José Llimerá (in Hermosilla Pla, 2011b). However, there is evidence that there were musical groups in Llíria from the middle of the eighteenth century onwards, and at the beginning of the nineteenth century, there was also "Military Music" and a "Chapel of Music" (Martín Montañés, 1994).

As for the origins of the Banda Primitiva, there are two documentary references from 1822 detailing the hiring of a musical group for religious events, i.e. street processions. These two historical documents are the *Libro de Deliberaciones de la Venerable Orden Tercera del Carmen de la Villa de Liria* (Book of Deliberations of the Venerable Third Order of Carmen of the Town of Llíria) (Orden del Carmen, 1822) and the *Libro de Entradas y Salidas del Convento de San Francisco* (Double-entry bookkeeping of the Convent of Saint Francis) (Orden Franciscana, 1821–1835). The first book details the cost of hiring "music" in mid-1822, this being equivalent to a musical group, and with the textual reference of "Música de bombo/Música del bombo" (i.e. bass drum music), to clearly differentiate it from chapel music, which was linked to the Parish Church of the Assumption (Asensi Silvestre, 2008; Llimerá in Hermosilla Pla, 2011b; Martín Montañés, 1994). On the other hand, the second document, linked to the old Saint Francis Convent, collects the oldest reference found so far of payment for the "music" (i.e. for the musical group) that dates back to March 1822, as well as other references from that same year for processions, such as the Easter procession and the reference to the procession of the Immaculate Conception, deeply rooted in the Raval neighbourhood or "Vila nova" (new town). This payment to the musical group was made periodically in subsequent years, for instance, on the occasion of Easter and Corpus Christi processions. It should be noted that the *Libro de Entradas y Salidas del Convento de San Francisco* prior to September 1821 has not been located, so it is unknown if there are previous references.

The relationship between Franciscan convents and the appearance of instrumental musical groups is a phenomenon that also occurred in other towns in the Valencian Region (Pérez-Jorge, 1951; Redacció ARA Multimèdia, 2013). This religious order did not have a chapel of musicians in their convents' churches, since its rules only contemplated singing in the Liturgy of the Hours. Then, it is reasonable to assert that this link may have been strengthened by the fact that they somehow promoted the development of musical groups by teaching music (Redacció ARA Multimèdia, 2013) and hiring the groups mainly for processions and other types of popular and religious acts related to the convent.

In the case of the Banda Primitiva, it was the Franciscan father Antoni Albarracín Enguídanos who promoted this initial seed documented at the beginning of the nineteenth century, mainly linked to the Franciscan convent of Llíria and centring above all on what we could call "Música de calle" (street music) or "Música del bombo" ("Bass drum music"), as mentioned above and which has lasted until today.

Based on the documents mentioned above, the first known performance of this group was registered in the first quarter of 1822. Therefore, its origin would have been a few years before that date, due to the time needed for the group to purchase the instruments required for playing and, mainly, to train the future musicians. This is probably the reason why the tradition takes 1819 as the beginning of this musical training, and why this year has been used by different authors as the starting date of the ensemble, e.g. Martín Montañés (1994).

This musical group continued its development in subsequent years, and it is in 1846 that it appears with the name of "Música Vella" (old music), as a result of the split of some of its members who formed a new group, the "Música Nova" (new music), as mentioned above. From 1848 onwards, the Música Vella became a full organised musical society that was governed by a Board headed by a Chairman.

In 1858, this Society appears under the name of "Banda Primitiva", also popularly known as the Clarín (Image 1), which maintains all the social and artistic heritage of the previous group (Llimerá Dus, 2011). Great musical artists have come out of this group, mainly in Spain and Europe including composers, conductors, instrumentalists and teachers in music schools, secondary schools and universities (Torres Castellano, 2006).

Currently, the society has over 1,000 members and develops its cultural activities through the different groups that make it up: the band, the youth band, the symphony orchestra, the choir and the theatre group, in addition to a music school that feeds all the society's groups.

6 Background of the Banda Primitiva de Llíria

The Banda Primitiva de Llíria is not only one of the oldest civic bands in Spain, but it is also one of the musical groups that have won the greatest number of awards in Europe. It is important to highlight that the Banda Primitiva won the first prize in the first Valencia community band contest in 1888 (Astruells Moreno, 2017) and it is the only one that has won this award in three consecutive centuries (Pelechà and Francés, 2016). It competes in the contest's highest category (Image 2), with over 30 first prizes and several honourable mentions, and its competitive spirit is one of the key factors of the band's resilience. Its ability to adapt and obtain positive results in the face of adverse situations is linked to the incentive effect that the competitive model of contests involves as they generate a whole system of rewards and moral incentives that encourage effort, as indicated by one of the society's members "everything that is not winning is losing. Going to a contest and finishing second is an absolute

Image 1 Group of Banda Primitiva musicians in the 1940s. *Source* Banda Primitiva de Llíria Archive, with permission

failure" (Informant 2). The most outstanding awards include (Banda Primitiva de Llíria, 2009b):

- The Gold Medal of the City of Llíria, awarded in 1962.
- The Gold Medal of the City of Kerkrade in the Netherlands, awarded in 1962.
- The Golden Trumpet of the Czechoslovak embassy in the Netherlands, awarded in 1966.
- The Gold Medal and Flag of the City of Kerkrade, awarded in 1966.
- The Silver Medal awarded by the Governor of Edinburgh in 1966.
- The Third Millennium Academy Award granted by the World Academy of Sciences, Technology, Education and Humanities in 2005.
- The 2012 Valencian Region Cultural Merit Medal, a distinction awarded annually by the Valencian Government to outstanding entities and individuals in the field of culture.

Since it was founded, the Banda Primitiva de Llíria has given innumerable performances that include concerts, parades and participation in diverse cultural events (Image 3). Some of the most relevant include the 1929 International Exhibition in

Image 2 The Banda Primitiva after the City of Valencia International Band Competition in 1913. *Source* Banda Primitiva de Llíria Archive, with permission

Barcelona, its 1984 performance at the Maurice Ravel Auditorium in Paris and the concert at the Municipal Theatre in Kortrijk (Belgium) to mark the 2nd WASBE World Congress. It has also performed in numerous charity events and international music promotion programmes in developing countries.

Image 3 Participation of the Banda Primitiva de Llíria in the Gracia Festival in Barcelona in the 1960s. *Source* Banda Primitiva de Llíria Archive, with permission

In 1976, the Banda Primitiva was hired by Spain's public television company (TVE) to perform in the programme *Directísimo*. In 1978, a live concert was recorded by TVE in Llíria's Main Square and another performance also took place at the Ministry of Culture Theatre in Madrid. For several years, the Banda Primitiva made recordings for the programme "Nuestras Bandas" on Valencian Television.

It has performed in practically all the main Spanish provincial capitals, as well as in various European countries, such as Germany, Belgium, France, the Netherlands and Switzerland (Banda Primitiva de Llíria, 2009b).

It was the first European band to perform in the USA, participating in the commemorative acts for Hispanic Day held in New York in October 1981 (Banda Primitiva de Llíria, 2009b). This performance had worldwide impact as it was broadcast by Univisión, TVE, RAI and other European television channels. In 1992, it returned to the USA for a tour of Los Angeles (to mark the 500th Anniversary of the Discovery of America) (Image 4). It was also the first European band to perform in China (Beijing and Shanghai) in 2004 (Banda Primitiva de Llíria, 2009b).

In addition to its principal music directors, the Banda Primitiva de Llíria has been led by some of the world's most prestigious conductors, such as Sergiu Celibidache, Desirée Dondaine, Odón Alonso, Rafael Frühbeck de Burgos, Plácido Domingo, Josep Pons, Miguel Ángel Gómez Martínez, Jan Molenaar, Manuel Galduf, Jan Cober, Luis Cobos and Rafael Sanz-Espert (Generalitat Valenciana,

Image 4 Banda Primitiva de Llíria playing in Pasadena's Rose Parade, California (USA), 1992. *Source* The Banda Primitiva de Llíria Archive, with permission

2012) (Banda Primitiva de Llíria, 2009b). Since November 2013, it has been led by Javier Enguídanos Morató (Banda Primitiva de Llíria, 2009b).

The Ateneo Musical y de Enseñanza Banda Primitiva de Llíria has made more than 50 audio, video and television recordings. Its performances have been broadcast on both state and foreign radio and television programmes.

Since 2008, the Banda Primitiva has actively collaborated with UNICEF. It has been a member of the WASBE since 2010 (Banda Primitiva de Llíria, 2009c).

7 The Banda Primitiva de Llíria as Intangible Cultural Heritage

It is important to remember that Intangible Cultural Heritage does not imply the absence of materiality but rather the incorporation of social practices, processes, knowledge and expressions, giving more importance to processes than to objects. The Banda Primitiva de Llíria is, therefore, the sum of the immaterial through music, the material with its instruments and scores, and of the cultural spaces inherent to it, such as its theatre-concert hall (Image 5).

Thus, the band is presented as a defined resource based on its social nature, highlighting the processes of creation, diffusion and the assignment of meaning.

Image 5 Banda Primitiva theatre-concert hall after a film showing in the 1960s. *Source* Banda Primitiva de Llíria Archive, with permission

Music makes more sense in that it is used, experienced, ritualised and identified by Edetans (inhabitants of Llíria) for whom belonging to the band is part of their family heritage (Informant 1). For its almost 500 federated musicians (band, youth band and orchestra), being a member of this musical society is a privilege, due to its historical background (Informant 2) (Image 6). In addition, the Banda Primitiva is presented as an open heritage resource, whose cultural outreach transcends the physical boundaries of Llíria, and is expanding thanks to the uses and values assigned to it not only by the Llíria society, but also by musicians from other nearby towns that have joined the band.

Currently, the Banda Primitiva de Llíria's main musical groups have over 180 musicians in the concert band and 75 musicians in the symphony orchestra. These can be broken down into the following categories (FSMCV, 2021b):

(a) Professional Musicians. Around 50% of the staff are professional musicians in various orchestras (e.g. the National Orchestra of Spain, the RTVE Symphony Orchestra, the Valencia Orchestra, the Principality of Asturias Symphony Orchestra, the Barcelona and National Orchestra of Catalonia, the Symphony Orchestra of Grand Liceo Theatre of Barcelona, the Symphony Orchestra of Bilbao, Symphony Orchestra of Castille and Leon, the Orchestra of Extremadura, the Symphony Orchestra of Madrid and the Symphony Orchestra of Malaga), professional wind bands (for example, the municipal bands of Valencia, Albacete, Alicante, Barcelona, Madrid, and Las Palmas de Gran Canaria), military bands (Band of the Royal Guard, Band of the Civil

Image 6 Participation of the Banda Primitiva de Llíria in the burial of one of its members in the 1960s. *Source* Banda Primitiva de Llíria Archive, with permission

Guard) and as teachers in the main Spanish public music schools (e.g. the music schools in Alicante, Castellon, Valencia, Castile-La Mancha, Granada, Madrid, Galicia, Jaen, Castellon, Valencia, and in many other schools in Valencian towns and across the rest of Spain). Some members of the society are also well-known professional conductors and composers.

(b) Non-professional musicians. Around 25% are amateur musicians who are engaged in other professional activities unrelated to music.

(c) Student musicians. Around 25% are young people who are studying music at different levels.

Sheet music is a fundamental heritage resource in a musical society. The works are usually played repeatedly or lent to other bands. The Banda Primitiva de Llíria's oldest sheet music in its archive dates back to 1917. Some sheet music may be older but has no date or signature (Informant 3) (Image 7).

The information available on these documents is the date and composer of the symphonic works. However, in most cases, the date on which they were transcribed is unknown, and the only information available is the name of the composer who wrote the work (Informant 3).

As a result of the fire that occurred in 1937 (Informants 2 and 5), the need arose to carry out an inventory of the recovered material heritage. Accordingly, in the 1950s, the archive was created to house a copy of each bought or original score that the

The Intangible Cultural Landscape … 83

Image 7 Oldest scores belonging to the Banda Primitiva de Llíria. *Source* Banda Primitiva de Llíria Archive (1919), with permission

Banda Primitiva has played. The state of conservation of the scores is good, and in 1994, the archive began to be digitalised (Informant 3).

The archive currently has 3,400 works on paper or in digital format, although after the recent discovery of new material (Informant 3), it is estimated that the archive will reach a total of 4,000 works (Informant 2). Thus, the musical society has a rich collection that includes scores for symphonic works, *zarzuelas*, pasodobles, procession marches and Easter marches. It should be noted that most of the works in the archive are symphonic orchestra scores which have been transcribed for concert bands, a task that was largely done by the musical director of the band at different times (Informant 3) or by donations (Informant 2). The musician who transcribed the greatest number of works was José María Malato (Image 8), the conductor of the Banda Primitiva de Llíria between 1960 and 1975, who contributed 30 works of approximately 20–30 min in length. It is important to emphasise that these works are registered in the SGAE (Informant 3) (Sanchis Rodenes & Malato Ruiz, 2004).

In the past, playing a transcribed work was considered to be a privilege. Currently, composers write directly for the wind orchestra (i.e. the band) and more importance is given to works expressly created for this kind of ensembles (Informant 3).

Finally, the Banda Primitiva, throughout its two centuries of history, has used different cultural environments to perform its activities. In the beginning, the main stage of the band was the street, where it played behind the main social, religious and festive events that took place in the town, such as parades and processions.

Image 8 Symphonic orchestra scores transcribed for the band by the director José María Malato in 1963 and 1966. *Source* Banda Primitiva de Llíria Archive (1919), with permission

Later, different municipal and private-owned venues were used, and it was not until practically 1950 that the Banda Primitiva acquired its own facilities.

The first theatre the Banda Primitiva used, known as the Español Theatre, was not owned by the Society and dates back to approximately 1895. This theatre closed in 1904, and the band moved to the former Saint Francis convent (Duran Martinez, 1995). Around 1915, different construction and refurbishment works were carried out in the Español Theatre so that the Society could relocate there; the theatre had a capacity of about 850 seats. The musical Society leased this facility on 15-year contracts, but none were fulfilled, which infers a tense relationship between the property's ownership and the Society. In this building, the Banda Primitiva played different *zarzuelas, sainetes* (skits) and staged theatrical representations (Images 9 and 10), generating great cultural vibrancy in the city that led many local authors and composers to premiere their works in this theatre. These included the premiere of *Emmanuel* in Christmas 1916 (Diario de Valencia, 1917). Films were also screened, and important concerts and plays by renowned groups and singers of the time were staged (Martín Montañés, 1994). This situation led successive boards of directors to consider acquiring the theatre, an opportunity that arose at the end of the Civil

Image 9 Former Español Theatre programme (1941). *Source* Miguel Blat Ibáñez Collection, IVC Musical Documentation Centre, with permission

Image 10 Front and back of an Español Theatre's Film Programme (1940). *Source* Miguel Blat Ibáñez Collection, IVC Musical Documentation Centre, with permission

War. From 1936 to 1939, the social club became headquarters and dining room for the front line that was located on the famous XYZ line (Mallench Sanz & Vicente Marco, 2018). In these years, the Banda was plundered, with instruments being sent to the front and to the different barracks for marches. Furthermore, in November 1937, the theatre suffered a fire that affected the extensive documentary and sheet music archive (Martín Montañés, 1994) (Informant 3).

At the end of the 1940s, the musical society managed to acquire the theatre (Image 11) and the social club premises (Banda Primitiva de Llíria, 1953a) (Image 12). Due to the condition of the theatre, the idea of improving all the society's

Image 11 Entrance to the former Español Theatre (1950). *Source* Banda Primitiva de Llíria Archive, with permission

facilities was soon raised, either by refurbishing them or by demolishing them and then building a new theatre. The debate on how to proceed with the theatre continued throughout the decade, with the positions in favour of refurbishment and demolition clashing at the various members' meetings. In the end, the decision to demolish the theatre prevailed, a stance that was not supported by the Chairman of the society at the time (Banda Primitiva de Llíria, 1953b). Finally, in June 1950, the works to build the new theatre began (Martín Montañés, 1994).

As we have explained above, the project for the new theatre lasted for almost a decade. Initially, the society occupied the former theatre, which had a smaller capacity. To increase its capacity, representatives of the musical society entered into negotiations with the owners of neighbouring properties to purchase them. This fact gives us an insight into the scope of the society's ambitions at that time in their quest to build a benchmark theatre in the Valencian Region.

After the Society members' decision to choose the demolition and construction project, a decision was made to ask the Monte de Piedad savings bank in Valencia for a loan of one million pesetas backed by the properties of the members who were willing to put them up as collateral (Banda Primitiva de Llíria, 1953c). It is important to remember that, despite the post-war situation of Llíria at that time, which

Image 12 Group of members together with the famous baritone Marcos Redondo, who gave several performances at the society, at the entrance to the social club in the former Español Theatre (1940s). *Source* Banda Primitiva de Llíria Archive, with permission

was a predominantly agricultural society that was dependent on ration cards until 1952 (Arco Blanco, 2006), and with a total population of less than 9,500 inhabitants (INE, 2020), the construction of a new theatre prevailed despite the difficulties. The social mass of the Banda Primitiva played a transcendental role in the construction of the building, as shown by the endorsement of the members and the selfless work that men and women linked to the Banda Primitiva put into the construction of the building, which meant huge cost reductions in the theatre's construction budget. Jobs that ranged from transporting materials with their own vehicles or carts, scaffolding and making fabrics meant important savings for the musical society. In addition to the direct cash contributions, different activities were also organised often involving women, such as the sale of lottery tickets and cakes to raise funds to help pay for the work. As a result of these contributions, it is estimated that the cost saving was over 650,000 pesetas in the construction of the new theatre (Banda Primitiva de Llíria, 1953a; Gasent-Blesa et al., 2019).

The theatre project was first assigned to Gimeno-Cruz, a renowned architect of the time who had worked in important towns such as Xativa, Gandia and Valencia. However, he did not finish the project because the society's Board decided to dispense with his services in 1950 due to issues and delays in the work. It is at this time that the figure of the prestigious architect Joaquín Rieta Síster (Banda Primitiva de Llíria, 1953d) became involved in the project. Rieta was the architect behind many other cultural buildings such as the Capitol and Tyris cinemas in Valencia (Herrera, 1983; IVAM and Generalitat Valenciana, 1998).

There are different hypotheses as to how Joaquín Rieta came into contact with the Banda Primitiva, though it was probably as a result of the relationship between him and Bartolomé Sabater, who had been the builder of some of Rieta's most important works in the city of Valencia. Sabater was a member of different society boards and was appointed by the Banda Primitiva to lead the construction of the new theatre-concert hall and the rest of the society's social club facilities, for over 1,200 people. The name of the architect Eduardo Alegre also appears in the documentation, who helped work against the clock (Gasent-Blesa et al., 2019).

Finally, Rieta was in charge of the work from around July 1950 until the theatre's opening on 23 September 1951, taking just 14 months to complete the project. As in the previous theatre, a broad range of cultural activities were offered including concerts, theatre and cinema (Image 13), attracting some of the most important European orchestras and soloists to the venue (Gasent-Blesa and Tándem Comunicación, 2019; Martín Montañés, 1994).

Subsequently, at the end of the twentieth century, both the theatre and the social club premises were renovated, and at the beginning of the twenty-first century, they were expanded to improve the quality of the facilities and offer more space for the music school including an auditorium with a hundred seats (the Malato Auditorium).

8 Resilience of the Banda Primitiva de Llíria as Intangible Cultural Heritage

The economic sustainability of this musical society is based on the diversity of its funding sources, including contributions from the local government, and income derived from the performances of the society's groups (mainly the band), its music school (Images 14 and 15), the fees paid by its members, the demand for music during festivities and even recent private sponsorship (Informant 2). In return for local government aid, the society performs various concerts and events in Llíria, as well as letting the town council use its theatre for different events, and other specific agreements with other public bodies.

The resilience capacity of the Banda Primitiva de Llíria comes largely from a diversified structure in which income is obtained from fees, public support, agreements and services. It is sustained mainly thanks "to the sense of identity" (Informant 2), and to the ability to symbolically represent the identity of the Edetans. These identity traits are what leads many of the members to undertake maintenance work for the Society, "the member is the one who maintains the band, when something is needed

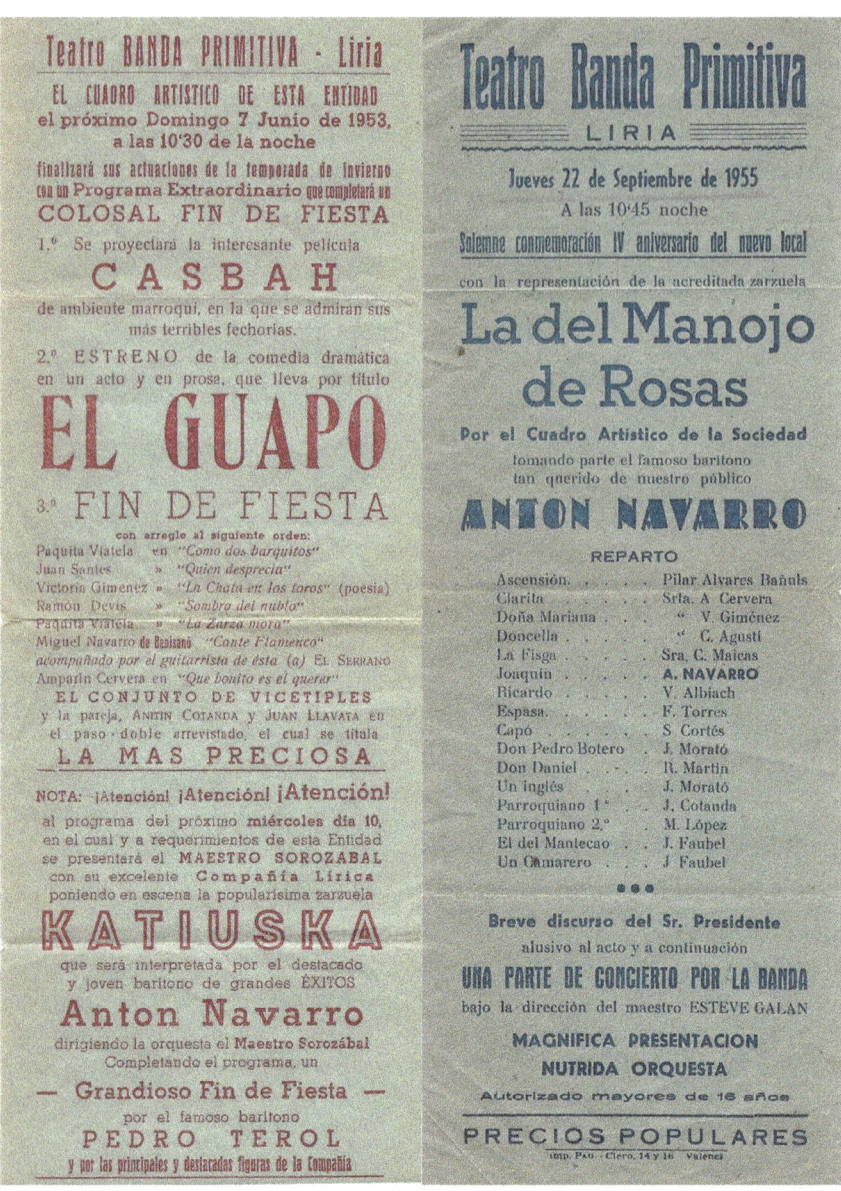

Image 13 New theatre film programme, 1953 and New theatre programme (1955). *Source* Miguel Blat Ibáñez Collection, IVAC Musical Documentation Centre, with permission

The Intangible Cultural Landscape ... 91

Image 14 Introduction of new technologies in the teaching methods of the Banda Primitiva de Llíria's music school. *Source* Banda Primitiva de Llíria Archive (2019), with permission

Image 15 Adapting teaching during the new health measures to prevent COVID-19, at the Banda Primitiva de Llíria's music school. *Source* Banda Primitiva de Llíria Archive (2020), with permission

they are usually there to provide it" (Informant 2), since "it is a feeling to be part of the Clarín, a feeling as though it were your home" (Informant 1).

The Banda Primitiva's ability to mobilise society was clearly reflected in 2019, when the Ateneo Musical y de Enseñanza Banda Primitiva de Llíria celebrated its bicentenary. This opportunity was used to put together a programme of events that turned the Banda Primitiva into a cultural hub in the Valencian Region (Image 16). The programme included the participation of the society in some of the most important musical events in Spain, such as the Bankia Orchestra Contest (Image 17), the International Band Contest in the city of Valencia (Image 18) and the Pamplona International Festival of Bands (IFOB). Different events were also organised in the theatre-concert hall such as concerts, *zarzuelas* and plays, and performances were given by some of the best groups in the country including the Spanish Radio Television orchestra, the Music Group of the *Inmemorial del Rey* No. 1 Regiment and the Valencia Municipal Band. They featured some of the most important international musical figures on the current scene such as the Venezuelan trumpeter Pacho Flores, the Valencian clarinetist José Franch and the Dutch conductor Jan Cober.

The Society's activities during 2019 were not limited exclusively to the musical field, but also included a cycle of conferences-concerts, a photography contest and workshops, mainly for school students but also for people with functional diversity (Una Il·lusió col·lectiva. El Teatre de Joaquín Rieta, 2020). These workshops brought

Image 16 Central event of the Banda Primitiva de Llíria's bicentenary celebrations. *Source* Banda Primitiva de Llíria Archive (2019), with permission

together more than 600 boys and girls, and adults with special needs and learning disabilities, who contributed their reflections on the social role of the Banda, as well as the analysis of its history and influence on the neighbourhood and town. At this point, the theatre-concert hall received special attention since it is one of the society's most impressive elements. Its construction took place in one of its peak moments as the nexus for the society of Llíria at the time. To commemorate this, an exhibition was organised in direct collaboration with researchers from the Universitat Politècnica de Valencia which brought a significant influx of visitors, including members of the Valencian Council of Culture, who held one of its plenary sessions at the theatre (Consell Valencià de Cultura, 2019). In addition, a documentary was produced in conjunction with the audiovisual company Tándem Comunicación which included interviews with people who worked altruistically in the construction of the theatre in 1950 and 1951 (Gasent-Blesa and Tándem Comunicación, 2019). Both public and private sponsors were obtained to fund these activities.

9 Conclusions

It is important to bear in mind that the phenomenon of music is an indicator of social change and an element that shapes different types of social identities (Asensi Silvestre, 2008). In the case of the Banda Primitiva de Llíria, also known as the Clarín,

Image 17 Banda Primitiva de Llíria's symphonic orchestra, directed by its principal conductor Juan José Aguado, during the 3rd Bankia Orchestra Contest in the Valencian Region at the Palau de les Arts Opera House in Valencia (2019). *Source* Banda Primitiva de Llíria Archive, with permission

it is presented as "the great cultural victory of the popular classes" (Informant 2). It is important to remember that in the nineteenth century a high percentage of the rural population that made a living from agriculture was practically illiterate. However, they knew how to read sheet music and knew the main classical music composers and their works (Informant 2). This musical movement constituted an unprecedented cultural event, as it brought important opportunities to the town, as well as validating the collective identity of Llíria, "there is no other town that has such a strong sense of identity" (Informant 2). As Alfonso Aijón describes, in the 1980s in Llíria, the farmers went to the fields with their work tools and their instruments so they could practise during their breaks (Martínez Luengo, 2017).

This work aims to offer a framework for reflection that helps Valencians to identify with one of the most vivid expressions of our cultural heritage, and thus promote the search for safeguarding and dissemination strategies that generate the sustainability of these heritage resources in the current situation of cultural and creative uncertainty.

Image 18 Tribute concert in the International City of Valencia Music Bands Contest to mark the Banda Primitiva's bicentenary at the Palau de les Arts Reina Sofía Opera House in Valencia (2019), with permission. *Source* Banda Primitiva de Llíria Archive, with permission

Acknowledgements This work has been carried out within the framework of the collaboration agreement between the Sociedad Ateneo Musical y de Enseñanza Banda Primitiva de Llíria and the Universitat Politécnica de Valencia, to develop the project entitled "Identity, political and economic analysis of the Banda Primitiva de Llíria as a changing and living social process". We would especially like to thank the support and material provided by the Banda Primitiva de Llíria. We would also like to thank Vicent Arastey Pablo for his valuable documentary contribution to this work, Carmen Pérez Sabater and Marisa Pérez Sabater for the review of this work, and Ana Peñarrocha, for providing us with the image of the Band in California.

Annexes

Interviews:

- Informant 1: Llíria chronicler. Date of interview: 26 April 2019. Interview conducted by Anna Palmira Rodríguez Llorens.
- Informant 2: Llíria historian and member of the Banda Primitiva de Llíria. Date of interview: 26 April 2019. Interview conducted by Anna Palmira Rodríguez Llorens.
- Informant 3: Llíria Archive Management collaborator and member of the Banda Primitiva de Llíria. Date of interview: 26 April 2019. Interview conducted by Celia José Herrando.

Archives:

- Banda Primitiva de Llíria Archive. Ateneo Musical y de Enseñanza Banda Primitiva de Llíria
- Miguel Blat Ibáñez Collection. IVC Music Documentation Centre, Valencian Government.

References

Arco Blanco, M. Á. d. (2006). «Morir de Hambre»: Autarquía, Escasez y Enfermedad En La España Del Primer Franquismo. *Pasado y memoria* (5), 241–258. http://hdl.handle.net/10045/5926 (February 13, 2021).

Asensi Silvestre, E. (2008). Sociabilidad e Identidad En Llíria: El Fenómeno Musical en un Municipio Valenciano (1822–1900). In *I Encuentro de Jóvenes Investigadores En Historia Contemporánea de La AHC*.

Astruells Moreno, S. (2017). El Certamen Internacional de Bandas de Música «Ciudad de Valencia» . *Estudios bandisticos. Wind Band Studies, 1,* 67–74. https://www.estudiosbandisticos.com/journal/index.php/estudiosbandisticos/article/view/29 (February 13, 2021).

Ayuntamiento de Llíria. (2019). Llíria, Declarada Ciudad Creativa de La Música por la Unesco. *Llíria City of music*. http://www.lliria.es/es/report/lliria-declarada-ciudad-creativa-musica-por-unesco (February 9, 2021).

Ayuntamiento de Llíria. (2020a). *La Ciudad*. http://www.lliria.es/es/content/ciudad (January 21, 2021).

Ayuntamiento de Llíria. (2020b). *Llíria City of music*. http://www.lliria.es/es/content/ciudad-de-la-musica-0 (December 11, 2020).

Badenes Masó, G. (1992). *Historia de La Música de La Comunidad Valenciana*. El mercantil valenciano.

Banda Primitiva de Llíria. (1953a). Libro de Actas de 1948–1953. *Archivo de la Banda Primitiva de Llíria* (Acta 178).

Banda Primitiva de Llíria. (1953b). Libro de Actas de 1948–1953. *Archivo de la Banda Primitiva de Llíria* (Acta 204).

Banda Primitiva de Llíria. (1953c). Libro de Actas de 1948–1953. *Archivo de la Banda Primitiva de Llíria* (Acta 208).

Banda Primitiva de Llíria. (1953d). Libro de Actas de 1948–1953. *Archivo de la Banda Primitiva de Llíria* (Acta 219).

Banda Primitiva de Llíria. (2009a). *Banda Primitiva de Llíria*. http://www.bandaprimitiva.org/index.php/es/ (April 25, 2020).

Banda Primitiva de Llíria. (2009b). *Historia - Banda Primitiva de Llíria*. http://www.bandaprimitiva.es/index.php/es/banda-primitiva-cs/historia-cs (February 10, 2021).

Banda Primitiva de Llíria. (2009c). *La Banda Primitiva de Llíria Presenta La Programación de Conciertos de Santa Cecília 2019 - Banda Primitiva de Llíria*. http://www.bandaprimitiva.org/index.php/es/sociedad1/noticias/678-programacion-stcecilia-2019 (April 25, 2020).

Bonet Rosado, H., Fortea Cervera, L., & Ripollés Adelantado, E. (2014). *Prehistory Museum of Valencia: Official Guide*. http://www.museuprehistoriavalencia.es/web_mupreva_dedalo/publicaciones/263/es (February 9, 2021).

Botella Nicolás, A. M. (2019). La Música Festera Como Patrimonio Inmaterial de la Humanidad. *Revista eWali de investigación antropológica, histórica, cultural y/o social en el entorno Mediterráneo* (1), 44–51. https://revistas.innovacionumh.es/index.php/eWali/article/view/355 (December 17, 2020).

Cardiel, J. G. (2017). Las Flautistas de Iberia. Mujer y Transmisión de La Memoria Social En El Mundo Ibérico (Siglos III-I a.C.). *Complutum, 28*(1), 143–162. http://dx.doi.org/10.5209/CMPL.58424 (February 9, 2021).

Casares Rodicio, E. (2006). *Diccionario de La Música Valenciana | ICCMU*.

Consell Valencià de Cultura. (2019). *Ple CVC a la Banda Primitiva de Llíria—CVC.*. https://cvc.gva.es/es/ple-cvc-a-la-banda-primitiva-de-lLlíria/ (February 10, 2021).

Cultural València. (2018). *Tradición de Las Bandas de Música. BIC*. https://cultural.valencia.es/es/patrimonio-cultural/tradicion-de-las-bandas-de-musica-bic/ (December 10, 2020).

Diario de Valencia. (1917). Teatros. *Biblioteca Virtual de Prensa Histórica* (2112), 3. https://prensahistorica.mcu.es/publicaciones/listar_numeros.do?busq_infoArticulos=true&submit=Buscar&busq_dia=&descendente=true&busq_idPublicacion=1000771&busq_mes=1&busq_anyo=1917&campoOrden=fechaPublicacion&posicion= (February 10, 2021).

Donat Zopo, J., & Gascó Martínez, F. (1973). *La Cova Del Cavall de Llíria (Valencia)*. Archivo de Prehistoria Levantina. http://www.museuprehistoriavalencia.es/web_mupreva_dedalo/publicaciones/481/es (February 9, 2021).

Duran Martinez, J. (1995). *Perfiles. Siluetas. Glosas de Mi Tierra.* Ajuntament de Llíria.

España. (1926). Real Decreto-Ley de 9 de Agosto de 1926. *Gaceta de Madrid* (227, de 15 de agosto). https://www.boe.es/datos/pdfs/BOE/1926/227/A01026-01031.pdf (December 11, 2020).

España. (1933). Ley Del Patrimonio Artístico Español. *Gaceta de Madrid* (145 de 25 de mayo), 1393 a 1399.

España. (1953). Decreto de 12 de Junio de 1953 Por El Que Se Dictan Disposiciones Para Formalización Del Inventario Del Tesoro Artístico Nacional. *Boletín Oficial del Estado* (182, de 1 de julio), 3993 a 3994. https://www.boe.es/buscar/doc.php?id=BOE-A-1953-9108 (September 24, 2020).

España. (1961). Decreto 1938/1961, de 22 de Septiembre, Por El Que Se Crea El Servicio Nacional de Información Artística, Arqueológica y Etnológica. *Boletín Oficial del Estado* (254 de 24 de octubre), 15217 a 15218.

España. (1978). Constitución Española. *Boletín Oficial del Estado* (311 de 29 de diciembre). https://www.boe.es/buscar/act.php?id=BOE-A-1978-31229 (December 11, 2020).

España. (1985). Ley 16/1985, de 25 de Junio, Del Patrimonio Histórico Español. *Boletín Oficial del Estado* (155, de 29 de junio). https://www.boe.es/buscar/act.php?id=BOE-A-1985-12534 (September 24, 2020).

España. (2007). Instrumento de Ratificación de la Convención para la Salvaguardia del Patrimonio Cultural Inmaterial, hecho en París el 3 de Noviembre de 2003. *Boletín Oficial del Estado* (31, de 5 de febrero), 5242 a 5248. https://www.boe.es/buscar/doc.php?id=BOE-A-2007-2382 (December 10, 2020).

España. (2015). Ley 10/2015, de 26 de Mayo, Para La Salvaguardia Del Patrimonio Cultural Inmaterial. *Boletín Oficial del Estado* (126, de 27 de mayo). https://www.boe.es/buscar/act.php?id=BOE-A-2015-5794 (December 10, 2020).

FSMCV. (2021a). *Las Sociedades Musicales de La Comunidad de Valenciana Son Declaradas Manifestación Representativa Del Patrimonio Cultural Inmaterial En España.* Noticias. https://fsmcv.org/es/actualidad/noticias/les-societats-musicals-de-la-comunitat-de-valenciana-son-declarades-manifestacio-representativa-del-patrimoni-cultural-immaterial-a-espanya (April 1, 2021).

FSMCV. (2021b). *Federació de Societats Musicals de La Comunidad Valenciana.* https://fsmcv.org/es/ (February 5, 2021).

Gasent-Blesa, J. L., Alcocer, P., Oliver, P., Baró, J. L., Iborra, F., & Guillén, I. (2019). *Exposició. Una Il·lusió Col·lectiva. El Teatre de Joaquín Rieta.* http://rieta.bandaprimitiva.es/index.php/val/ (April 25, 2020).

Gasent-Blesa, J. L., & Tándem Comunicación. (2019). *Vídeo-Documental Una Ilusión Colectiva - Fragmento. España.* https://www.youtube.com/watch?v=XlEWeyGg7TA (February 10, 2021).

Generalitat Valenciana. (1998). Ley 4/1998, de 11 de Junio, Del Patrimonio Cultural Valenciano. *DOGV* (3267 de 18 de junio). https://www.boe.es/buscar/act.php?id=BOE-A-1998-17524&p=20170411&tn=2 (December 10, 2020).

Generalitat Valenciana. (2011). Orden 1/2011, de 12 de Julio, de La Conselleria de Turismo, Cultura y Deporte, Por La Que Se Declara Bien Inmaterial de Relevancia Local La Tradición Musical Popular Valenciana Materializada Por Las Sociedades Musicales de La Comunidad Valenciana. [2011/8]. *DOGV* (6571 de 22 de juio). http://www.dogv.gva.es/portal/ficha_disposicion_pc.jsp?sig=008384/2011&L=1 (December 10, 2020).

Generalitat Valenciana. (2012). Decreto 147/2012, de 5 de Octubre, Del Consell, por el que concede la Distinción de la Generalitat al Mérito Cultural a la Banda Primitiva de Llíria. [2012/9286]. *DOGV* (6878 de 8 de octubre). http://www.dogv.gva.es/datos/2012/10/08/pdf/2012_9286.pdf (February 10, 2021).

Generalitat Valenciana. (2018). Decreto 68/2018, de 25 de Mayo, Del Consell, Por El Que Se Declara Bien de Interés Cultural Inmaterial La Tradición Musical Popular Valenciana Materializada Por Las Sociedades Musicales de La Comunidad Valenciana. *DOGV* (8308 de 1 de junio). https://www.dogv.gva.es/es/eli/es-vc/d/2018/05/25/68/ (December 10, 2020).

Hermosilla Pla, J. (2011a). Historia Contemporánea. In *Llíria, Historia, Geografía y Arte: Nuestro Pasado y Presente* (pp. 251–369). Facultat de Geografia i Història Universitat de València.

Hermosilla Pla, J. (2011b). Historia de La Música. In *Llíria, Historia, Geografía y Arte: Nuestro Pasado y Presente* (pp. 211–248). Facultat de Geografia i Història Universitat de València.

Hermosilla Pla, J. (2011c). Historia Medieval. In *Llíria, Historia, Geografía y Arte: Nuestro Pasado y Presente* (pp. 109–152). Facultat de Geografia i Història Universitat de València.

Hermosilla Pla, J. (2011d). Historia Moderna. In *Llíria, Historia, Geografía y Arte: Nuestro Pasado y Presente* (pp. 155–208). Facultat de Geografia i Història Universitat de València.

Hermosilla Pla, J. (2011e). Llíria Durante El Periodo Romano y La Antigüedad Tardía. In *Llíria, Historia, Geografía y Arte: Nuestro Pasado y Presente* (pp. 49–106). Facultat de Geografia i Història Universitat de València.

Herrera, J. M. (1983). *Joaquín Rieta Sister, Arquitecto Valenciano: 1897–1982*. Colegio Oficial de Arquitectos de Valencia.

INE. (2020). Valencia/València: Población Por Municipios y Sexo. *Cifras oficiales de población de los municipios españoles: Revisión del Padrón Municipal. Resultados*. https://www.ine.es/jaxiT3/Datos.htm?t=2903#!tabs-tabla (January 21, 2021).

IVAM and Generalitat Valenciana. (1998). *La Ciudad Moderna: Arquitectura Racionalista En Valencia*. Valencia.

Llimerá Dus, J. J. (2011). Asociacionismo: El Ateneo Musical y de Enseñanza, Banda Primitiva de Llíria. In *Llíria, Historia, Geografía y Arte Nuestro Pasado y Presente* (pp. 343–353).

Mallench Sanz, C., & Vicente Marco, B. (2018). Línea XYZ. El Impenetrable Muro de Levante. *Desperta Ferro: Contemporánea* (27), 36–42.

Martín Montañés, R. (1994). *Historia Músico-Social Del Ateneo Musical y de Enseñanza : Banda Primitiva de Llíria*. https://www.musicaalallum.es/es/materiales/historia-banda-primitiva-de-lLlíria/ (February 9, 2021).

Martínez Luengo, J. (2017). Alfonso Aijón: 'No Hay Orquesta Importante Que No Tenga Solistas Españoles' | El Cultural. *EL CULTURAL*. https://elcultural.com/Alfonso-Aijon-No-hay-orquesta-importante-que-no-tenga-solistas-espanoles (February 13, 2021).

Ministerio de Cultura y Deporte. (2011). *Plan Nacional de Salvaguardia Del Patrimonio Cultural Inmaterial*. http://www.culturaydeporte.gob.es/planes-nacionales/planes-nacionales/salvaguardia-patrimonio-cultural-inmaterial.html (December 10, 2020).

Orden del Carmen (presumed). (1822). *Libro de Deliberaciones de la Venerable Orden Tercera del Carmen de la Villa de Llíria*. [Manuscrito] Archivo la iglesia de la Asunción de Nuestra Señora, hoja 9 vuelto, Llíria.

Orden Franciscana (presumed). (1821–1835). *Libro de Entradas y Salidas del Convento de San Francisco (Llíria)*. [Libro de Cuenta y Razón o de Ingresos] Archivo del Reino de Valencia, Libro 339 (1821-09-15–1835-08-14), Valencia.

Pelechà, P., & Francés, M. (2016). *Documental "50 Aniversari 1r Premi de La Banda Primitiva a Kerkrade."* YouTube. https://www.youtube.com/watch?v=bSu4wckOZgQ (February 10, 2021).

Pérez-Jorge, V. (1951). *La Música En La Provincia Franciscana de Valencia.*

Rausell Köster, P. (2013). Las Sociedades Musicales 2020. In *III Congreso General de Sociedades Musicales 2013 Resumen Ejecutivo.* http://www.uv.es/cursegsm/PDF/IIICSMCVRE.pdf (June 22, 2019).

Redacció ARA Multimèdia. (2013). Qui per Frà, Qui per Germà, Tot Lo Món Es Franciscà. *ARA Multimèdia.* https://www.aramultimedia.com/qui-per-fra-qui-per-germa-tot-lo-mon-es-francisca-2 (February 13, 2021).

Rodríguez Lorenzo, G. A. (2014). *The Banda Municipal de Música de Madrid* [The Municipal Band of Madrid] (pp. 1–17).

Rosado, H. B., Parreño, C. M., & Martín, A. M. (2008). Iron age landscape and rural habitat in the Edetan Territory, Iberia (4th-3rd Centuries BC). *Journal of Mediterranean Archaeology, 21*(2), 165–189. https://journal.equinoxpub.com/JMA/article/view/874 (February 9, 2021).

Sanchis Rodenes, E., & Malato Ruiz, J. M. (2004). *Josep M. Malato Ruiz: Un Il.Lustre Músic Tarragoní.* Tarragona.

SGAE. (2020). *Las Bandas de Música de La Comunidad Valenciana Serán Declaradas Patrimonio Cultural Inmaterial.* SGAE. http://www.sgae.es/es-ES/SitePages/EstaPasandoDetalleActualidad.aspx?i=4451&s=5 (December 10, 2020).

Tormo-Esteve, S. (2018). The Roman baths of Mura in Llíria (Valencia): Study applied to the thermal functionality of the Roman thermal complex—Dialnet. In I. Cabrera Fausto (Ed.), *Reactive proactive architecture* (pp. 372–377). UPV[Scientia]. https://gdocu.upv.es/alfresco/service/api/node/content/workspace/SpacesStore/ad88c844-156b-4743-889f-2123acbcaa84/6472.pdf?guest=true

Torres Castellano, M. (2006). *Llíria, Cuna de Músicos.* Ajuntament de Llíria.

UNESCO. (1989). *Recomendación Sobre La Salvaguardia de La Cultura Tradicional y Popular.* http://portal.unesco.org/es/ev.php-URL_ID=13141&URL_DO=DO_TOPIC&URL_SECTION=201.html (April 11, 2020).

UNESCO. (1998). Resoluciones. In *Actas de La Conferencia General. 29ª Reunión. París, 21 de Octubre - 12 de Noviembre de 1997* (pp. 1–140). https://unesdoc.unesco.org/ark:/48223/pf0000110220_spa (December 11, 2020).

UNESCO. (2001). *Proclamación de Las Obras Maestras Del Patrimonio Oral e Inmaterial de La Humanidad (2001–2005).* https://ich.unesco.org/es/proclamacion-de-obras-maestras-00103 (September 24, 2020).

UNESCO. (2003). *Convención Para La Salvaguardia Del Patrimonio Cultural Inmaterial.* http://portal.unesco.org/es/ev.php-URL_ID=17716&URL_DO=DO_TOPIC&URL_SECTION=201.html (April 11, 2020).

UNESCO. (2008). *Las Listas del PCI y El Registro de Buenas Prácticas de Salvaguardia.* https://ich.unesco.org/es/listas (December 10, 2020).

UNESCO. (2019). *#WindowsOfMusicAndHope in Llíria, UNESCO Creative City of Music.* https://en.unesco.org/news/windowsofmusicandhope-lliria-unesco-creative-city-music (December 11, 2020).

UNESCO. (2020). Creative Cities. *Creative Cities Network.* https://en.unesco.org/creative-cities/ (December 17, 2020).

Uriel, D. (1946). Bosquejo Histórico de La Música En Llíria, Excluyendo Los Tiempos Actuales. *Saitabi revista de la Facultat de Geografia i Història, 4*(20–21), 95–109.

Open Access This chapter is licensed under the terms of the Creative Commons Attribution 4.0 International License (http://creativecommons.org/licenses/by/4.0/), which permits use, sharing, adaptation, distribution and reproduction in any medium or format, as long as you give appropriate credit to the original author(s) and the source, provide a link to the Creative Commons license and indicate if changes were made.

The images or other third party material in this chapter are included in the chapter's Creative Commons license, unless indicated otherwise in a credit line to the material. If material is not included in the chapter's Creative Commons license and your intended use is not permitted by statutory regulation or exceeds the permitted use, you will need to obtain permission directly from the copyright holder.

Music for the Moors and Christians Festivities as Intangible Cultural Heritage: A Specific Genre for Wind Bands in Certain Spanish Regions

Daniel Catalá-Pérez and Gabino Ponce-Herrero

1 Introduction

The history of wind bands and their music is a history of vindication (Dubois et al., 2013, p. xi; Reily & Brucher, 2013, p. 3). More than a hundred years ago, Parès (1898) wrote in the prologue of the first treatise on band orchestration that "… we must seek the necessary means to give fanfare music, as well as harmony music (wind bands), the relevance that belongs to them, and we hope to show that, like the symphony orchestra, they can translate the composer's inspirations and be worthy of his attention …". Just three years ago, Pascual-Vilaplana (2017) spoke about the situation in Spain stating that if "the presence of a band in important music festivals continues to surprise us even in 2017, this is symptomatic of the road ahead. […] The normality should be to take advantage of our professional wind bands, both civil and military, as well as the amateur ones, to better use their artistic potentialities. […] we must be able to make ourselves visible, to assert ourselves with our work and not to give into ignorance".

The lack of knowledge about the history of wind bands and the economic, cultural and social importance that their activity implies, has become a serious obstacle to the correct management of the huge and highly valuable cultural heritage that the entire wind band music corpus represents in Spain (Cipollone Fernández, 2016, p. 162). In fact, the international bibliography barely includes studies on the vast repertoire that this Spanish music segment constitutes (studies such as Reily & Brucher, 2013, which ignore the Spanish case, are a clear example), nor is there a review in Spanish

---

D. Catalá-Pérez (✉)
Universitat Politècnica de València, Valencia, Spain
e-mail: dacapre@ade.upv.es

G. Ponce-Herrero
Universidad de Alicante, Alicante, Spain
e-mail: gabino.ponce@ua.es

© The Author(s) 2021
B. de-Miguel-Molina et al. (eds.), *Music as Intangible Cultural Heritage*, SpringerBriefs in Economics,
https://doi.org/10.1007/978-3-030-76882-9_7

of the international wind music repertoire. In fact, in Spain, research on wind band music has usually been included in the study of popular folklore or has been limited to monographic studies on some specific wind bands, composers and, to a lesser extent, directors (Cipollone Fernández, 2016, pp. 159–161).

Wind band music and the role of wind bands require an in-depth study beyond beliefs, customs and clichés in order to give them the value they deserve. This is especially relevant for two reasons: the wind band model in Spain, as we will see later, differs from other international models as it is a means for the cultural expression of local identity and autonomy, given that bands are intricately linked to local popular festivities (Dubois et al., 2013, p. xiv). In addition, the management and organisation model of these bands through the so-called musical societies, which constitute one of the most important association movements in Spain, is also especially interesting.

Their relevance in the Valencian Region is especially salient, with a total of 555 musical societies in a territory with 542 municipalities, 71% of which have less than 5,000 inhabitants. (INE, 2020). Such is the importance that these entities have for Valencian society that the Regional Government declared them as an Asset of Intangible Cultural Interest for the Valencian Region in 2018, thus giving them special protection.[1] The link between musical societies and popular Valencian festivals such as *Fallas* and *Foguere*s is significant, but it is especially relevant in terms of the Moors and Christians festivals. These are, in turn, one of the most important festive events in the region, present in at least 181 municipalities (Alcaraz Santonja, 2019). In 2015, they were declared as an Intangible Asset of Local Relevance by the Valencian Government.[2]

Since the end of the nineteenth century, the symbiosis of both phenomena has created an exclusive musical repertoire for these popular festivals that include several thousand compositions. Thus, numerous authors have demanded recognition for the specific genre of wind band music (Botella-Nicolás, 2014; Pascual-Vilaplana, 2001). In the case of the Valencian Region, given the importance of the musical society phenomenon, some studies have focused on their functioning, their role in Valencian society and their economic impact (e.g. Rausell, 2018). Additionally, authors such as Botella-Nicolás (2014, 2018) and Cipollone-Fernández (2017) have focused on the study of the musical corpus that has emerged as a result of this relationship and its cultural and artistic value. However, in general terms, there is a clear need to delve deeper into these research areas (Rausell, 2018, p. 5).

This chapter makes a brief approach to the origins and evolution of both wind bands and the Moors and Christians festivals, especially in the Valencian context, tracing the lines that connected both phenomena at a specific moment in history. The indissoluble relationship that has united them since then has created a musical genre that has not only become one of the most recognisable signs of Valencian society's

---

[1] DECREE 68/2018, of 25 May, of the Valencian Regional Government, under which the Valencian popular musical tradition materialised by the musical societies of the Valencian Region is declared to be of intangible cultural interest.

[2] ORDER 50/2015, of 13 May, of the Valencian Region's Ministry of Education, Culture and Sports, declaring the Moors and Christians festivities of the Valencian Region as an Intangible Asset of Local Relevance.

identity, but also a treasure of its intangible cultural heritage, and a fundamental part of the economic activity of musical societies in the context of what certain authors call the ecosystem of the Moors and Christians cluster (Martínez Puche et al., 2019).

2 The Moors and Christians Festivities: A Global Phenomenon with Local Peculiarities

2.1 Origin and Spread of the Phenomenon of Moors and Christians Festivals

The Moors and Christians festivals in their multiple modalities constitute a complex phenomenon, whose study and comprehensive understanding require an approach from diverse perspectives including anthropology and ethnology (Martínez Pozo, 2015), sociology (Alcaraz Santonja, 2019), ethnography and history (Domene Verdú, 2018), economy (Latorre Ruiz, 2019; Perles Ribes & Díaz Sánchez, 2019), literature (Domene Verdú, 2018) and musicology (Botella-Nicolás, 2018; Cipollone-Fernández, 2017). A factor that further increases the complexity of phenomenon must also be added: the expansion of Moorish and Christian festivals throughout the world (Catalá-Pérez, 2017).[3]

Brisset Martín (2001) affirms that "in essence, the Moors and Christians festival consists of a popular theatre performance [...], expressing the fight between the side of the heroes (the Christians) and that of the enemies (the Moors) for the possession of a collective good, through actions and / or discussions" (Brisset Martín, 2001). In any case, the origin of these representations comes from the dramatisation through dance of the fights between Moorish and Christian troops which were performed in royal celebrations to commemorate certain victories during the time known as the Reconquest in the Iberian Peninsula (Amades, 1966; Brisset Martín, 1988; Catalá-Pérez, 2012).

For many researchers, the first historical reference mentioning a battle dramatised as a dance took place in Lleida in 1150 during the wedding of Ramon Berenguer IV, Count of Barcelona, and Petronila, daughter of Ramiro I, King of Aragon (Brisset Martín, 1988). For other authors, the first reference is the representation of a naval battle between two galleys of Christians and Saracens that Peter IV, known as the Ceremonious, organised in 1373 to commemorate the visit of his future daughter-in-law Martha de Armanyac to Barcelona (Massip, 2015). However, the truth is that these representations were already contemporaneous with the battles they commemorated

---

[3] In fact, in recent years, there has been interest in approaching the study of Moors and Christians festivals from an international perspective. Proof of this is the different scientific events that have been organised in recent years: the International Congress on the *Komedya Fiesta* (as the Moors and Christians festivals are known in the Philippines) held in 2008 at the University of the Philippines-Diliman and the different international congresses held in Spain in 2010 (in Ontinyent, Valencia), 2016 (University of Alicante) and 2018 (Villena, Alicante) (Catalá-Pérez, 2017).

and up to the fifteenth century they were organised almost exclusively on the occasion of royal festivals.

Even so, from the late fourteenth century onwards, the Catholic Church saw an excellent evangelising vehicle in the representation of the confrontation between the Christian and Muslim faith. Soon, elements of this confrontation were incorporated into certain religious festivities such as Corpus Christi (certain dances are still preserved in some localities) including the representation of moralising plays on the victory of the Christian faith over Islam. In addition, with the arrival of the Spanish in America, many of these plays were used in their missions to Christianise the new territories (Catalá-Pérez, 2012). The truth is that with the expansion of the Spanish empire, the Moors and Christians festival reached many of the territories under their dominion, sometimes in Europe as royal celebrations, and in overseas territories as tools of religious-cultural imposition. In certain places, the festival continues to be celebrated whilst in others it has disappeared, although testimonies of its existence remain. In other places, the original representations evolved until they became rituals that differ significantly from the original.[4]

2.2 The Valencian Model of the Moors and Christians Festivities

In the Spanish context, the end of the sixteenth century and especially the seventeenth century saw the Moors and Christians become the most widespread festivity. On the one hand, the changes caused by the Counter-Reformation and the Council of Trent (1545–1563) introduced acts related to the historical representation of the battles between Moors and Christians in the formerly, solely religious, patron saint festivities in numerous localities. Before this time, the Moors and Christians festivities had been organised by local guilds. In addition, the participation of local militias[5] in the festivities became widespread. The militias accompanied the patrons in the processions firing their arquebuses and also represented each of the sides (Moors and Christians) in simulated battles (Domene Verdú, 2018, p. 564). Additionally, from the seventeenth century onwards, in addition to the Reconquest, the festivities began to represent other historical events such as the attacks by Berber pirates on the shores of the Mediterranean and the expulsion of Spanish Moorish descendants in 1609.

---

[4] Various authors (Brisset Martín, 1988, 2001; Domene Verdú, 2018; Martínez Pozo, 2015; Warman Gryj, 1972) have studied the influences and historical circumstances that have marked the evolution of the primitive representations of Moors and Christians until they became, over the centuries, one of the most widespread festive manifestations in the world, present, in one way or another, on the five continents (Catalá-Pérez, 2017).

[5] The term militia refers to "a type of armed organization made up of men to defend a territory, serve as a reserve force, maintain public order or fight for a specific political cause" (Contreras Gay, 1992, p. 75). The participation of the militias in the patron saint festivities of numerous localities became widespread as of the sixteenth century, with this participation even becoming compulsory by way of military manoeuvres to keep said militias trained (Martínez Pozo, 2015, p. 118).

Thus, the representations of Moors and Christians became popular and spread to the smaller towns. At the end of the seventeenth and early eighteenth centuries, we can already find references to some of the most well-known Moors and Christians festivals in the Valencian Region, such as those of Alcoy and Villena (Domene Verdú, 2018).

In the nineteenth century, a series of circumstances ended up shaping the Moors and Christians festival as we know it today in the Valencian Region, differentiating it from the festive model in other regions. Firstly, the division of the participants on the Moors and Christians sides into *comparsas* or *filaes* was generalised.[6] Secondly, thanks to the creation of these *comparsas* or *filaes*, the military parades that had already been performed by the militias took on special relevance.

The greater variety of characters made these parades more spectacular and, at the same time, generated the need to add new pieces to the musical repertoire to accompany the *comparsas*, beyond the traditional military marches. Thus, at the end of the nineteenth century, the first specific compositions for these parades were written (Cipollone-Fernández, 2017), helping the *entradas*[7] to gain prominence in the festive calendar. At this point, the Valencian Moors and Christians festival model was configured as it remains to this day: historical events (discussions and simulated battles) alternating with religious events (processions and masses) and military acts (parades and firing of arquebuses) (Domene Verdú, 2018, p. 56). Institutions such as the National Union of Festive Entities (UNDEF, in its Spanish acronym), made up of towns and cities that celebrate this festive model, have been working to preserve them since 1974. In this sense, the Valencian Regional Government recognised their importance to Valencian society by declaring them as an Intangible Asset of Local Relevance in 2015.

Finally, the most recent history of the Moors and Christians festivities in Valencia is fundamentally marked by three events: first, the great expansion of the festival since the beginning of the current democratic period, especially in the northern area of the province of Valencia; secondly, the search for the features that characterise the identity of each population through the recovery of local history; and finally, the design of the Moors and Christians festival as a visual and musical spectacle beyond its historical significance, which has led many municipalities to only incorporate processions such as the *entrada* into their festive calendar. Thus, Alcaraz Santonja

---

[6] The *comparsas* or *filaes* are groups of people who represent different historical identities, sometimes linked to the historical origin of the representations (e.g. Templars, Hospitallers, Crusaders, etc., on the Christian side, and Berbers, Mudejars, Bedouins, etc., on the Moorish side). Certain events of a political nature (the growth of certain ideologies), military nature (e.g. the Carlist wars, the War of Independence and the Morocco war) and a cultural nature (Romanticism and the arrival of the cinema) led to the appearance of *comparsas* such as smugglers, farmers, students, corsairs, buccaneers and musketeers who, far from being medieval stereotypes, represent idealised figures of the historical moment in which they were included in the representations. This fact accentuated the popular nature of the Moors and Christians festivals.

[7] *Entrada* (literally, entrance, in English) is the name given to the parades of the Moorish and Christian troops, symbolising the moment in which they "enter" the town to start the fight.

Table 1 Formal types of Moors and Christians festivals in Spain

Formal Type	Description
Modern Moors and Christians festival	A type that originated at the end of the eighteenth century and the middle of the nineteenth century which is characterised by a sequence that includes historical, religious and military acts, and by an organisational structure divided into *filaes/comparsas* that go beyond the traditional division of Moors and Christians
Entrada of Moors and Christians as a festive complement	A type that has emerged in recent decades based on a single act, the *Entrada* of Moors and Christians, which is embedded within the patron saint festivals of a town or neighbourhood, but which does not respond to the dramatic sequential logic of events that characterise the previous model
Traditional Moors and Christians festival: comedies and simulacra	A type that has maintained its basic ritual sequence unaltered for decades and even centuries, to which the main two features identified in the previous types have not been incorporated: the *Entrada* and the division of the festival into *filaes/comparsas*
Moors and Christians dances	A type that consists of a spoken dance where a ritual confrontation between two groups of dancers is symbolised and includes a fight between Moors and Christians in one of its parts

Source Authors' own, based on Alcaraz Santonja (2019)

(2019) classified the Moors and Christians festivals in Spain according to their formal characteristics, differentiating between the four types shown in Table 1.

Alcaraz Santonja (2019) identified 359 festive representations of Moors and Christians based on these formal types, distributed by region, as shown in Table 2. This shows that the most widespread formal type is that of the modern festival in the Valencian Region. In addition, the Valencian area is also where the *entrada* type as a festive complement has developed the most. These are precisely the two models where wind bands are especially important elements in the festival.

The festival as we know it in Valencian towns is capable of creating a social environment around it in which people can find personal development. It is also a source of cultural, economic and social wealth for any town where it is celebrated. Accordingly, the Moors and Christians festivities in the twenty-first century are based on new contemporary values that go beyond classic traditional, religious and historicist ones (Martínez Pozo, 2015):

- The feeling of belonging to a community.
- The cyclical nature of the festivities, as opposed to the routine of everyday life, has the virtue of endowing them with their own time, which can imply an acceleration or a deceleration of experiences.

Table 2 Distribution of the festive representations of Moors and Christians in Spain

Region	Province	Formal types				Total	
		Modern Festival	"Entrada" as Complement	Traditional Type	Dances		
Andalusia		8	2	66		**76**	
Aragon			2	2	34	**38**	
Castile La Mancha		4	2	11	1	**18**	
Castile and Leon				4	1	**5**	
Catalonia		1	1	4	9	**15**	
Madrid			1			**1**	
Valencian Region	Alicante	53	23		3	**79**	**181**
	Castellon		6		1	**7**	
	Valencia	38	53	2	2	**95**	
Extremadura			1			**1**	
Galicia				5		**5**	
Balearic Islands		1		3		**4**	
Canary Islands				2		**2**	
Navarre					1	**1**	
Basque Country					1	**1**	
Murcia		10		1		**11**	
Totals		**115**	**91**	**100**	**53**	**359**	

Source Authors' own based on Alcaraz Santonja's data (2019)

- Festivals are a means of integration that helps to create strong bonds of friendship.
- They are a social phenomenon, a space for multi- and intercultural coexistence between people, men and women of different social origins, generations, cultures and even religions.
- They are festivals that have been adapted to the different historical moments and different territories where they are rooted.

In addition, in the case of the Valencian model's festivals, despite the search for historicity, postmodernity has opened a path to a game of fantasy where the visual and performing arts have taken on great importance. The influence of historical, epic and, above all, fantastic cinema, as well as contemporary theatre, has created mythological figures that have become part of the parades giving them a new appearance and culture, without neglecting the inheritance received from many centuries of history.

In this context, the Moors and Christians festivals are a very relevant phenomenon from an economic point of view for the Valencian Region, firstly, from the perspective of their impact on the municipalities in which they are held. In this sense, some studies have quantified this impact at exceeding €20 million in a town like Alcoy (Latorre Ruiz, 2019), €8 million in Elda (Pedrero Rico, 2016) and €5.5 million in Calpe (Perles Ribes, 2006), and secondly, as a cluster which authors such as Martínez Puche et al. (2019) referred to as "the ecosystem of the Moors and Christians festivals" in which they identified microclusters, such as festive crafts, which include elements that also generate economic activity such as monumental heritage, accommodation, regulations, music, the participatory nature of festivals, gastronomy, history and identity, communication and marketing.

3 Wind Bands: Approach to Their Origin and Evolution

According to the British National Federation of Musical Societies (2017), "a wind band is composed of instruments where the sound is produced by making a column of air vibrate inside the instrument, so that's wind and brass instruments". It could be thought "that the word wind means just woodwind instruments, but in this case the word wind refers to the way the sound is produced, rather than being a short version of the word woodwind". In a very simple way, a wind band is basically an orchestra with the strings removed and saxophones added. Obviously, the correct definition is more complex, but there is no standardised line-up for wind bands, so parts are often omitted and/or included in other parts.

In the woodwind section, "the wind band uses extra clarinet parts to replace the missing strings, with multiple players on each part […]. There are flute, piccolo, oboe and bassoon parts, and the addition of four saxophone parts who help to fill in the middle register harmonies that come between the high woodwind/brass melody instruments and the very low bass instruments". The brass section includes the standard orchestral line-up of horns, trumpets, trombones and tubas. Cornets and/or extra trumpets are usually required, and euphoniums are added to help the saxophones complete the middle harmonies. Two tubas, often doubling in octaves, create a strong bass line. Finally, in addition to wind instruments, there is also a percussion section. Typically, a wind band percussion section will have more to do than in a symphony orchestra, and the players are required to switch between several instruments in the same piece. One of the main characteristics of wind bands is that they are great for outdoor performances, because their sound carries easily without additional amplification (National Federation of Musical Societies, 2017).

The origin of wind bands in the Middle Ages comes from references to groups of minstrels that played in religious acts and the instrumental groups that served as court entertainment (Rhodes, 2007). Later, in the Renaissance, the *Alta Capella* formation was common as a group destined to perform at public events and large religious celebrations, generally outdoors (Mayor Catalá, 2011). But since the *Alta Capella,* there was no type of grouping formed exclusively by wind instruments that enjoyed popularity until the appearance of the *Harmoniemusik* in the Classicism of the eighteenth century (Rhodes, 2007).

The nineteenth century was, without a doubt, one of the most important and fruitful periods in the development and birth of wind bands, as we know them today. There were two clear influences: firstly, the aforementioned *Harmoniemusik* movement, which diversified the instrumental wind groups of the eighteenth century, both in the ceremonies of European aristocratic houses and in the most popular festive manifestations, and secondly, the military bands that aroused national sentiment and moved the masses, which popularised them among the population at mass events. The major influence that the Band of the Turkish Janissaries had in this regard in Europe should be mentioned here (Reily & Brucher, 2013).

In the Spanish state, from the end of the nineteenth century, popular wind bands began to be created, in many cases, by retired military musicians. These bands known as "militia bands" were dressed in military-style suits. Documentation exists of the creation of popular wind bands such as the Wind Music Band of Irún (1784), that of Xativa (Valencia, 1800), Muro (Alicante, 1801), Manresa (Barcelona, 1815), *Banda Primitiva de Llíria* (Valencia, 1819), *Banda de Éibar* (1831) and the *Banda de Bergara* (1832) (Pascual-Vilaplana, 2020).

The evolution of wind instruments, the invention of new ones (such as those patented by Adolph Sax in 1845) and the interest generated by highly relevant composers, led wind and percussion bands to advance. Their roles ranged from performing religious music in temples and/or processions, to dancing and symphonic concerts, as well as performing arrangements of symphonic works, operas and *zarzuelas*. However, symphonic music for bands in Spain was relegated to suites for waltzes and polkas, with no relevant echo in concert halls. The melodies of overtures, operas, symphonies and *zarzuelas* were well known in towns thanks to wind bands, and not to their orchestral originals. This relegated the use of original wind band music which, although it was composed, had little influence beyond regionalist and folkloric works. Hence, the importance of the appearance in the nineteenth century of the widespread band movement that emerged in the Valencian Region: the music for the Moors and Christians festival (Pascual-Vilaplana, 2011).

3.1 The Valencian Model of Musical Societies

Musical societies make up an association movement known mainly as a wind band movement, given that the wind band is the original artistic unit around which each musical society is shaped. The management model of bands through musical societies is widely extended in Spain. According to data from the Spanish Confederation of Musical Societies (COESSM, in its Spanish acronym)[8] at the end of 2019, there were 14 regional federations in Spain representing a total of 1,513 musical societies, with around 112,000 musicians (most of them amateurs), over 120,000 students in their music schools and more than 1,000,000 members. Table 3 shows the number of musical societies by regional federations and autonomous regions in Spain.

The Valencian Region has the largest number of musical societies in Spain (more than a third of the total, according to the table above) and constitutes an internationally studied model (Cohen, 1997, 1999; Molle, 2008). Valencian musical societies participate in cultural events and celebrations of all kinds throughout the year. They

---

[8] Information available on the COESSM website (https://coessm.org/).

Table 3 Number of Spanish musical societies by region

REGION	REGIONAL FEDERATION	SOCIETIES
Andalusia[a]	*Federación de Bandas de Música de Andalucía*	337
Aragon	*Federación Aragonesa de Sociedades Musicales y Escuelas de Música Amateurs*	50
Asturias[b]		14
Balearic Islands	*Federación Balear de Bandas de Música y Asociaciones Musicales*	37
Canary Islands	*Federación Gran Canaria de Bandas de Música*	52
	Federación Tinerfeña de Bandas de Música	
Cantabria[b]		1
Castile La Mancha	*Federación Castellano-Manchega de Sociedades Musicales (incluye la Federación Provincial de Bandas de Guadalajara)*	91
Castile and Leon	*Federación Castellano-Leonesa Asociaciones Musicales, Bandas y Escuelas Música*	27
Catalonia	*Federación Catalana de Sociedades Musicales*	44
Valencian Region	*Federación de Sociedades Musicales de la Comunidad Valenciana*	555
Extremadura	*Federación Extremeña de Bandas de Música*	63
Galicia	*Federación Gallega de Bandas de Música Populares*	88
Rioja[b]		1
Madrid	*Federación Regional de Sociedades Musicales, Comunidad de Madrid*	27
Murcia	*Federación de Bandas de Música de la Región de Murcia*	40
Navarre	*Federación Navarra de Bandas de Música*	59
Basque Country[b]		27
TOTAL		**1,513**

Source Authors' own taken from https://coessm.org/
[a]Information about Ceuta and Melilla is included
[b]There are no regional federations in these autonomous regions

are a clear example of a successful social project that is not only long-lasting in time but is constantly growing, and it is a social movement considered by the Regional Government as a characteristic feature identifying Valencian society. Accordingly, in 2018, the popular Valencian musical tradition materialised by musical societies was declared as an Asset of Intangible Cultural Interest of the Valencian Region.

Currently, Valencian musical societies have much more than just a wind band as their only artistic unit. They also have other groups such as orchestras, chamber orchestras, big bands, choirs and other instrumental groups. In any case, and although it is obvious that the wind band is the most relevant group in their artistic spectrum in the vast majority of cases, the Valencian Region Federation of Musical Societies

(FSMCV, in its Spanish acronym) has established a definition of the concept of musical society:

- Private entities with an adequate and sufficient social mass.
- Non-profit entities, with a legal form, legally constituted and recorded in a public registry, with independent control over their governance and management.
- Entities related to the society in which they operate and with which they work closely.
- Entities with a music school that guarantees the sustainability of the musical project.
- Entities with at least one working artistic musical group.

Valencian musical societies are open societies. In recent years, they have adapted to the times without losing their essence and they have become not only sociocultural spaces, but also places for the exchange of ideas and opinions among people of all social, cultural and religious classes. This is one of the keys to their survival as an association movement. In addition, musical societies, and wind bands as their main artistic unit, carry out a fundamental task to preserve Valencian musical heritage through different activities:

- The educational activities that enable them to nurture their musical project and to provide flexible, high-quality musical training to neighbouring society.
- The many cultural activities that they organise, which include concerts, exchange programmes with other municipalities, participation in competitions, participation in European projects and the organisation of festivals.
- Their fundamental contribution to Valencian society's way of life through their connection to traditional local festivals. The Moors and Christians festivities cannot be understood without the wind bands in their *entradas*. The *Fallas* and the *Fogueres* festivals cannot be understood without street band music, together with other types of festivities in which parades are always accompanied by wind bands.

All these activities also have a significant economic impact that makes musical societies an important resource for local development as they mobilise an important cultural industry. In fact, the direct economic effects of musical society activities were close to €40 million in 2018, representing 0.04% of the Valencian Region's GDP (Rausell, 2018, p. 29).

However, this economic importance is even greater if we take into account, firstly, the multiplier effect they have on other industries and related activities (music publishing, recording industry, musical instrument industry, education) with the expenditure of the musical societies, and, secondly all the "grey economy" generated around their activities that is not reflected in official figures. Thus, taking into account the indirect and induced effects, the total economic impact would be around €60 million (Rausell, 2018, p. 29). Therefore, musical societies can also be considered as a cultural cluster that has an enormous amount of material and human resources which, when they are actively encouraged, have very high transformation effects on the territory.

4 Moors and Christians Festivals and Music: An Inseparable Pair

As commented above, Moors and Christians' representations were born as simulated danced battles and, as such, were accompanied by music. In fact, current Moors and Christians' dances are still accompanied by popular melodies interpreted with traditional instruments (GEA, 2010). Likewise, if we refer to former representations of Moors and Christians in the form of religious theatre, it was also common to accompany such representations with music to accentuate the educational and moralising sense of the representation (Lara Coronado, 2012).

At present, the musical genre for Moors and Christians is classified into liturgical works, processional works, martial works and evocative works (Cipollone-Fernández, 2017, pp. 227–228). The bulk of the repertoire consists of martial works, the type of music that is used basically in the *entradas*, which includes the three fundamental compositional modalities of the genre, i.e. pasodobles,[9] Moorish marches and Christian marches (Botella-Nicolás, 2014, p. 333).

Although it is difficult to establish exactly when the transition from military music to specific music for Moors and Christians occurred (today, there are certain Moors and Christians festivals in which military marches are still played), there are references from the time when wind bands begin to participate in the Valencian Moors and Christians festivities. Thus, in 1817 in Alcoy, the Band of the National Militia Battalion was the first wind band to participate in an *entrada* of Moors and Christians (Botella-Nicolás, 2014, p. 334). Given that the first compositions created for the Moors and Christians festivities appeared in the last quarter of the nineteenth century, it is highly probable that the repertoire of the parades at that time included other types of popular compositions such as polkas, mazurkas and *habaneras*, in addition to military music (Botella-Nicolás, 2014, p. 334).

In the second half of the nineteenth century, there were already some Moors and Christians festivals with a complex structure of *comparsas* or *filaes* and with a clear interest in increasing the spectacular nature, splendour and ostentation of their parades (Ariño Villarroya, 1988, p. 40). This fact, together with the liking for orientalism and the exotic nature of musical romanticism, was key factor for the apparition of the first compositions designed for the Moors and Christians in the last third of the nineteenth century (Oriola Velló, 2012, p. 96). There is an open debate between authors who consider different composers from Alcoy (Alicante) as the precursors of music for Moors and Christians (Botella-Nicolás, 2013; Mansanet Ribes, 1987) and others who point out previous contributions by composers from other locations (Domene Verdú, 2018; Ferrero Pastor, 1987). In any case, the first compositions were basically pasodobles and Moorish marches. Although there are precedents from the late nineteenth century, the Christian marches developed later.

---

[9] Among the *pasodobles* composed for the Moors and Christians festival, there is one piece that has transcended the limits of the genre and has become a festive hymn throughout the world. It is the work known as *"Paquito el Chocolatero"*, composed by Gustavo Pascual Falcó from Cocentaina (Alicante) in 1937.

The first Christian march dates back to 1958, but its habitual use in *entradas* did not become widespread until at least two decades later.

There are five basic stages in the development of music for Moors and Christians. During the time of musical classicism (1899-1936), the festival assimilated music, that is, there was a period of adaptation between both elements. In the renovation period (1940-1957), styles were refined and the modern Moorish march appeared, with a more leisurely pace (Cipollone-Fernández, 2017, p. 220). Later, with the first Christian march, the golden age of Moorish and Christian music began and lasted until 1980. During this period, composers were concerned with historicity. Thus, religious overtones were introduced into the Christian march, and the warlike character of the compositions in which percussion takes centre stage was accentuated, giving a certain epic tone to the compositions.

Finally, the contemporary period of festive music, which began in 1980, is a particularly complex period in the musical sphere in which new musical languages have been incorporated. There is greater freedom in terms of musical structure and the influence of other genres, especially film music, is evident, with adaptations of numerous soundtracks. Special attention is paid to concert activity, and traditional instruments have been included in compositions and performances (Cipollone-Fernández, 2017, p. 223).

In this current period, composition activity has boomed, unusually, to the point that it has become difficult to absorb all the musical creations. One of the few formal approaches that have been made to catalogue the Moors and Christians festival repertoire dates back to 2001 and is estimated at more than three thousand works composed expressly for this festival, of which 1,936 have been catalogued (Francés Sanjuán, 2001). Since then, the number of compositions has grown exponentially. In any case, the figures suggested are part of the information put together by enthusiasts of the genre who have voluntarily collected data from personal websites and through social network profiles. Thus, according to these sources, the repertoire could be made up of around 6,000 compositions at present.[10] Some musical societies are performing the interesting and much-needed task of compiling and digitising their musical databases.[11] Institutions such as UNDEF have also tried to promote the creation of a musical archive in this area. One of the organisations that are working to showcase this very important cultural heritage is the Association of Composers of Music for Moors and Christians (ACMMICC, in its Spanish acronym), claiming that it is a genre that should have the same consideration as any other musical genre, both by the general public and by the composers and performers themselves (Pascual-Vilaplana, 2001).

---

[10] Some examples of these informal sources of information are websites (https://www.musicafestera.com/obres or https://www.acordesfesteros.es/) and social network profiles (e.g. https://www.youtube.com/c/morosycristianos/featured).

[11] This is the case, for example, of the *Corporación Musical Primitiva de Alcoy* (http://primigest.primitivadealcoi.org/archivo).

5 Final Reflections on the Economic, Cultural and Social Relevance of Music for the Moors and Christians Festivals

Valencian musical tradition and, in particular, that of wind bands, as well as the Valencian Moors and Christians festivals, make up two cultural phenomena of an immaterial nature whose need for protection has been recognised by the Regional Government. Music for the Moors and Christians festivals is the element that links both phenomena, with implications from an economic, social and cultural point of view.

On a social level, the Valencian Region has the greatest presence of musical societies and Moorish and Christian festivals in Spain in which bands play a fundamental role in certain acts (*entradas* and other parades). Ironically, the moment in which the modern Moors and Christians festival finally established its festive model and when *comparsas* became widespread coincides approximately with a boom in the number of civil bands across Spain, though this was more significant in the Valencian region. Thus, the incorporation of wind bands into the Moors and Christians parades became commonplace, generating a relationship between bands and *comparsas* that transcends the commercial, especially in terms of the consolidation of music for Moors and Christians as a genre and its dependence on both parties for optimum development. In this sense, UNDEF and FSMCV signed a collaboration agreement in 2011 that recognised, on the one hand, the importance of the Moors and Christians festivals for the subsistence of a large number of musical societies in the Valencian Region, and on the other, the fundamental contribution of these musical societies to the Moors and Christians festivals, recognising the wind bands and the music for these festivals as being fundamental and essential elements of them (UNDEF-FSMCV, 2011). Over time, both association movements have consolidated their roles as a point of contact between the different strata of society, becoming unique and differentiating features of the Valencian Region and a backbone of it.

In addition to the volume of the repertoire, the cultural and artistic value and impact that music has on Moors and Christians in the Valencian region are undeniable. The problem arises from the need for genuine recognition of this cultural and artistic value from all the stakeholders involved, whether we are talking about the general public, participants in festivals, the composers or the musicians themselves. Thus, the aforementioned UNDEF-FSMCV agreement recognised music for Moors and Christians as one of the most genuine manifestations of Valencian music, and established the unquestionable need for its study and promotion, granting it the dignity it deserves within the artistic and cultural context (UNDEF-FSMCV, 2011). Thus, the measures proposed in the agreement to respect the cultural and artistic value of the compositions included the formalisation of contracts with legally recognised musical societies. This aimed to guarantee proper training of the musicians, away from the intrusionism of certain informal groups of musicians formed ad hoc for specific events. It also established the need to have musical advisers on the *comparsas'* boards of directors, providing guidance on the vast possibilities of the existing repertoire, the minimum conditions that a band must have in order to adequately perform a work, etc.

From an economic point of view, the major impact that the Moors and Christians festivals and the activity of musical societies have on the Valencian economy has been corroborated. In this sense, a large part of the economic flows that are generated around the Moors and Christians festivals in a town is linked to the hiring of bands for musical accompaniment in parades or for the celebration of other activities which include concerts, recreational performances and recordings. In fact, the participation of the wind bands in the Moors and Christians festivals is not limited to *entradas*. It is very common for various Moors and Christians concerts to be organised in each town throughout the year, some of which are recorded. It is also common for wind bands to entertain brotherhood lunches and dinners. These activities make up a fundamental part of many musical societies' sources of funding. Studies on the economic impact of musical societies include the analysis of this kind of activities but not only in the case of music for Moors and Christians (Rausell, 2018, pp. 27–28). Therefore, it would be a very interesting exercise to disaggregate these data by genre in order to ascertain the real economic impact of this type of music. In fact, we hope that this work can provide a starting point to intensify research into music for the Moors and Christians festivals as intangible cultural heritage and its social and economic implications.

References

Alcaraz Santonja, A. (2019). *La dimensió lúdica i transgressora de les festes de moros i cristians. Sociabilitat, diversió i espectacle en l'origen, evolució i expansió d'una festa moderna (1839–2018)*. Universitat d'Alacant - Universidad de Alicante, Alicante.
Amades, J. (1966). *Las Danzas de Moros y Cristianos*. Instituto de Estudios Ibéricos y Etnología Valenciana.
Ariño Villarroya, A. (1988). *Festes, rituals i creences*. Institució Valenciana d'Estudis i Investigació.
Botella-Nicolás, A. M. (2013). Orígenes de la música en las Fiestas de Moros y Cristianos de Alcoy. *Revista de Folklore, 372,* 28–38.
Botella-Nicolás, A. M. (2014). La música de Moros y Cristianos como patrimonio cultural y artístico. Posibilidades de trabajo en aula. *Tejuelo. Didáctica de La Lengua y La Literatura Educación, 9,* 331–349.
Botella-Nicolás, A. M. (2018). *La riqueza de la música de Moros y Cristianos como patrimonio artístico y cultural II*. Sociedad Latina de Comunicación Social.
Brisset Martín, D. E. (1988). *Representaciones rituales hispánicas de conquista*. Servicio de Publicaciones and Universidad Complutense de Madrid.
Brisset Martín, D. E. (2001). *Fiestas hispanas de moros y cristianos* (p. 17). Gazeta de Antropología: Historia y significados.
Catalá-Pérez, D. (2012). La fiesta de Moros y Cristianos: herencia cultural compartida entre España y América Latina. In A. Colomer Viadel (Ed.), *América Latina, globalidad e integración I* (pp. 407–427). Ediciones del Orto.
Catalá-Pérez, D. (2017). La Fiesta de Moros y Cristianos y su extensión en todo el mundo: una visión abierta e integradora. In G. Ponce Herrero (Ed.), *Moros y Cristianos: un patrimonio mundial.*

VI Congreso Nacional y I Internacional sobre la Fiesta de Moros y Cristianos. (pp. 29–45). Publicacions Universitat d'Alacant.

Cipollone-Fernández, A. (2017). *Miguel Villar González (Sagunto 1913 – Gandía 1996) y su aportación a la música de las fiestas de Moros y Cristianos*. Universidad de Alicante.

Cipollone Fernández, A. (2016). Gestión del patrimonio inmaterial: la presencia de la música para banda en los estudios académicos españoles. In E. Cutillas Orgilés (Ed.), *La diversidad en la investigación humanística: V Jornadas de Investigación de la Facultad de Filosofía y Letras de la Universidad de Alicante* (pp. 157–166). Compobell.

Cohen, R. S. (1997). *The musical society community bands of Valencia, Spain: A global study of their administration, instrumentation, repertoire and performance activities*. Northwestern University.

Cohen, R. S. (1999). Community ensemble music as a means of cultural expression in the Catalan-speaking autonomies of Spain. In D. Dougherty & M. M. Azevedo (Eds.), *Multicultural Iberia: Language, literature and music* (pp. 230–251). University of California Press.

Conselleria de Educación Investigación Cultura y Deporte. DECRETO 68/2018, de 25 de mayo, del Consell, por el que se declara bien de interés cultural inmaterial la tradición musical popular valenciana materializada por las sociedades musicales de la Comunitat Valenciana (2018).

Contreras Gay, J. (1992). Las milicias en el Antiguo Régimen. Modelos, características generales y significado histórico. *Chronica Nova. Revista de Historia Moderna de La Universidad de Granada, 0*(20), 75–104. https://doi.org/10.30827/CN.V0I20.2741.

Domene Verdú, J. F. (2018). *Las fiestas de moros y cristianos de Villena*. Universidad de Alicante.

Dubois, V., Méon, J.-M., & Bart, J.-Y. (2013). *The sociology of wind bands. Amateur music between cultural domination and autonomy. The sociology of wind bands*. Routledge. https://doi.org/10.4324/9781315552644.

Ferrero Pastor, J. M. (1987). ¿Juan Cantó Francés o Camilo Pérez Laporta? *Actas del I Centenario de la Música Festera de Moros y Cristianos, Cocentaina, 1982* (pp. 221–225). UNDEF.

Francés Sanjuán, P. J. (2001). El repertorio en la música para las fiestas de moros y cristianos (1882–2000). In *I Encontre de Compositors de Música per a Moros i Cristians*. Muro d'Alcoi.

GEA. (2010). *Dance*. Retrieved 16 September 2019, from http://www.enciclopedia-aragonesa.com/voz.asp?voz_id=4549.

INE. (2020). *Número de municipios por comunidad autónoma y provincia y tamaño de municipio*. Retrieved 17 November 2020, from https://www.ine.es/jaxi/Datos.htm?path=/t20/e245/p04/provi/l0/&file=0tamu001.px#!tabs-tabla.

Lara Coronado, J. (2012). *La educación moral en los autos sacramentales del siglo XVI en Nueva España. Perfiles educativos* (Vol. 34). Instituto de Investigaciones sobre la Universidad y la Educación, UNAM.

Latorre Ruiz, Á. (2019). *Análisis de la influencia socioeconómica de las fiestas de moros y cristianos en la ciudad de Alcoy*. Universidad Politécnica de Valencia.

Mansanet Ribes, J. L. (1987). Aportación al origen y evolución de la música festera. *Actas del I Centenario de la Música Festera de Moros y Cristianos, Cocentaina, 1982* (pp. 207–217). UNDEF.

Martínez Pozo, M. Á. (2015). *Moros y Cristianos en el Mediterráneo Español: antropología, educación, historia y valores*. Gami Editorial.

Martínez Puche, A., Martinez Puche, S., Ribera Sevilla, P., & Esteban Buendía, J. (2019). Microcluster de la confección y alquiler de trajes de moros y cristianos en el contexto de los sistemas productivos tradicionales. El corredor del Vinalopó (Alicante) ¿Una transición resiliente? In *International Conference on Regional Science*. Asociación Española de Ciencia Regional.

Massip, F. (2015). Los Doce Pares de Francia en el México de hoy: vasos comunicantes con la teatralidad popular europea. In M. Ruiz Bañuls, J. L. V. Ferris, & B. Aracil (Eds.), *América Latina y Europa : espacios compartidos en el teatro contemporáneo* (p. 539). Visor.

Mayor Catalá, B. (2011). Introducción a la Harmoniemusik. *Sinfonía Virtual. Revista de Múascia Clásica y Reflexión Musical*, (21).

Molle, M. (2008). *Approche Ethnologique et Ethnomusicologique de l'Univers des Bandas.* Université Libre de Bruxelles.

Oriola Velló, F. (2012). Música i festa. Les societats musicals i les grans festivitats del poble valencià. In M. L. Del Cerro (Ed.), *Arriben bandes. Les societats musicals valencianes* (pp. 75–104). Museu Valencià d'Etnologia.

Parès, G. (1898). *Traité d'instrumentation et d'orchestration à l'usage des musiques militaires d'harmonie et de fanfare.* Henry Lemoine & Cie.

Pascual-Vilaplana, J. R. (2001). La música de moros i cristians: història, vigència i defensa d'un gènere bandístic. In *Simpòsium de música festera de la Vall d'Albaida.*

Pascual-Vilplana, J. R. (2017). *La normalización de la cultura bandística.* Retrieved 17 November 2020, from https://www.pascualvilaplana.com/es/articulos/art/normalizacion-cultura-bandistica/39/pag/7.

Pascual-Vilaplana, J. R. (2011). *Las bandas de música: vehículo de cultura para el siglo XXI.* Retrieved 17 November 2020, from https://www.pascualvilaplana.com/es/articulos/art//15/pag/11.

Pascual-Vilaplana, J. R. (2020). *Tiempos de bandas. 125 Aniversario de la BM de Bilbao (1895–2020).* Retrieved 17 November 2020, from https://www.pascualvilaplana.com/es/articulos/art/tiempo-bandas/68/pag/1.

Pedrero Rico, G. (2016). *Repercusión económica de las fiestas de moros y cristianos de Elda.* Universidad de Alicante.

Perles Ribes, J. F. (2006). Análisis del impacto económico de eventos: una aplicación a fiestas populares de proyección turística. *Cuadernos de Turismo, 17,* 147–166.

Perles Ribes, J. F., & Díaz Sánchez, E. (2019). Reestimación del impacto económico de las fiestas populares de proyección turística a través de metadatos provenientes de la telefonía móvil: Calp, un ejemplo de aplicación. *PASOS Revista de Turismo y Patrimonio Cultural, 17*(5), 947–961.

Rausell, P. (2018). *Estructura, dimensión e impacto económico de las sociedades musicales.* Universitat de València - FSMCV - Econcult.

Reily, S. A., & Brucher, K. (Eds.). (2013). *Brass bands of the world: Militarism, colonial legacies, and local music making. Brass bands of the world: Militarism, colonial legacies, and local music making.* Routledge. https://doi.org/10.4324/9781315569895.

Rhodes, S. L. (2007). *A history of the wind band.* Lipscomb University.

The National Federation of Musical societies. (2017). *An introduction to: Wind bands.* Retrieved 22 November 2020, from https://www.makingmusic.org.uk/resource/introduction-wind-bands.

UNDEF-FSMCV. (2011). *Convenio UNDEF - FSMCV para el establecimiento de unos acuerdos de mínimos que regularán las relaciones entre ambas entidades y sus asociados.*

Warman Gryj, A. (1972). *La danza de Moros y Cristianos.* Secretaría de Educación Pública.

Open Access This chapter is licensed under the terms of the Creative Commons Attribution 4.0 International License (http://creativecommons.org/licenses/by/4.0/), which permits use, sharing, adaptation, distribution and reproduction in any medium or format, as long as you give appropriate credit to the original author(s) and the source, provide a link to the Creative Commons license and indicate if changes were made.

The images or other third party material in this chapter are included in the chapter's Creative Commons license, unless indicated otherwise in a credit line to the material. If material is not included in the chapter's Creative Commons license and your intended use is not permitted by statutory regulation or exceeds the permitted use, you will need to obtain permission directly from the copyright holder.

The Impact of the COVID-19 Pandemic on Musical Societies in the Valencian Region, Spain

María Ángeles Carabal-Montagud, Guillem Escorihuela-Carbonell, Virginia Santamarina-Campos, and Javier Pérez-Catalá

1 Musical Societies in the Valencian Region

Musical societies in the Valencian Region are complex structures that include symphonic bands, music schools, choirs and orchestras. They are responsible for the transmission of knowledge and offer comprehensive training based on an association-type organisation. Some of them have a main band and another youth or children's band.

According to data from the Valencian Region Federation of Musical Societies, there are over 1,100 bands, over 600 educational centres, over 40,000 musicians, 60,000 students and 200,000 members in the Valencian Region's musical societies (Las Provincias, 2020).

The social fabric that is generated by these societies is very extensive, given that their legacy is part of local culture and heritage, and they are linked to the creative and cultural industries. Not only are they centres where knowledge is imparted, but they also write methods and develop musical learning computer programmes for their schools, thus generating new ICT learning methodologies.

M. Á. Carabal-Montagud (✉) · V. Santamarina-Campos
Universitat Politècnica de València, Valencia, Spain
e-mail: macamon@crbc.upv.es

V. Santamarina-Campos
e-mail: virsanca@crbc.upv.es

G. Escorihuela-Carbonell
ISEACV, Institut Superior D´Ensenyances Artístiques de La Comunitat Valenciana, Valencia, Spain
e-mail: gescorihuela@florida-uni.es

J. Pérez-Catalá
Centre Artístic Musical, Moncada, Asociación Musical, Rocafort and Societat Artística, Alginet, Spain

© The Author(s) 2021
B. de-Miguel-Molina et al. (eds.), *Music as Intangible Cultural Heritage*, SpringerBriefs in Economics,
https://doi.org/10.1007/978-3-030-76882-9_8

1.1 Historical Introduction to Musical Societies

The origins of these bands in the Valencian Region lie in religion, recreational centres, casinos and military institutions (Almeria, 2014).

The first written evidence of the existence of national military bands appeared in 1792 (Vell, 2014). Some of the bands in the region were created using instruments from the First Carlist War period, between 1833 and 1840. An example is the Banda La Lira de Titaguas (Image 1), founded in 1840, which revealed that "when the government forces arrived to reduce the Carlist forces, they abandoned in their flight the band's musical instruments that they were carrying. These were picked up by a neighbour called Blas Portolés, a potter and violinist, who took advantage of this circumstance to found a small band in the town of Titaguas" (Exm. Ayuntamiento de Titaguas, 2020).

The military bands disseminated knowledge by giving music classes throughout the nineteenth and twentieth centuries, and were the first to combine musical education with the band function. Ecclesiastical music chapels were also a source of transmission and music teaching in the nineteenth century, along with private music teaching centres for the civilian population (Fernández Vicedo, 2010).

There have been bands in the Valencian Region for over two centuries. These include the Banda de Muro, created in 1801 (Unió Musical Muro, 2020), and the Banda Primitiva de Llíria, founded in 1819 (Ateneu Musical i d´Ensenyament, 2019).

Image 1 Sueca municipal band founded in 1847, in a photo from 1921 (*Source* Ferri Chulio [1983])

According to Ruiz de Lihory in *La música en Valencia, Diccionario biográfico y crítico,* at the end of the nineteenth and beginning of the twentieth centuries, a number of bands were founded in villages near the city of Valencia, led by the maestro José Balanzá Herrera. "He organized and directed several municipal bands in different towns, such as Silla, Alcacer, Picassent and others, leaving in all of them a multitude of pieces expressly written [...]" (Ruiz de Lihory, 1903). Since then, the number of bands has grown constantly, with groups being formed throughout the twentieth century (Image 2), such as the Banda de Torrefiel, in 1913 (Centro Instructivo Musical Banda de Torrefiel, 2020) and the Unió Musical de Albaida "l'Aranya", in 1923 (Unió Músical D'Albaida "L'Aranya", 2020).

Some of today's musical societies are a merger of older bands. An example is the Union Musical de Sax, founded in 1929, which joined forces with the Sociedad Musical la Primitiva and the Banda de Música La Moderna, both from the nineteenth century.

There are also cases of old bands that disappeared and have been re-founded, such as "Sueños de Artista" in Almedijar, founded in 1912 and re-founded in 2012 (Unión Musical "Sueños de Artista", 2020), and the Unión Musical de Caudiel, which was founded in 1891, disappeared in 1954 and returned in 1991 (InfoPalancia, 2016).

During the twenty-first century, newly created musical societies have continued to appear, such as the Banda Tendetes in the city of Valencia, founded in 2000 (Centro Musical Tendetes, 2020), and the Musical Centre Històric de València, in 2016.

Image. 2 Silla municipal band, in 1927 (*Source* Les Bandes de Música de Silla [2006])

The bands' association model is based on that of the *Federació de Societats Musicals de la Comunitat Valenciana* (FSMCV). The Valencian Region Federation of Musical Societies was created in 1968 whilst the Valencian Music Law was approved in 1988, to "promote the development of musical societies and the evolution of their music schools" (Almeria, 2014). According to its own statement, the FSMCV defines as itself "a non-profit entity whose objective is to unite its member associations in order to promote, disseminate and dignify the hobby, teaching and practice of music, by promoting the associations and providing civil society with means of development and cultural organisation" (FSMCV, 2020). Furthermore, it represents and defends the interests of musical societies in their relations with public and private institutions, and it requests, channels and advises them on the financial aid available and the subsidies granted by national and international institutions, and contributes to their cultural and educational work.

1.2 Musical Society Functions

Musical societies are self-governing. They follow an association-based model and must be sustainable, build trust and persist over time. They must ensure the management and effectiveness of resources (employees and volunteers), creativity and culture; training and promotion of musical talent (transmission of knowledge), social dynamics and a reflection of the community, and innovation and connection with the world and the impact derived from changes (III General Congrés de Societats Musicals de la Comunitat Valenciana, 2013). The adaptability of these entities to events has been very surprising, as the recent COVID-19 pandemic has shown.

One of the main functions of musical societies is the conservation and continuity of the documentary heritage of their bands, which is one of the symbols of Valencian identity.

Musical societies are funded by membership fees, the sale of lottery tickets and other types of subsidies given by local and regional government, such as contracts and collaboration agreements to perform concerts, musical exchanges with other cities, musical performances at folk festivals and other contracts for musical performances such as the *Fallas* and Moors and Christians festivals. Another source of income is provided by subsidies for music schools, which are granted by the Valencian Regional Government's General Directorate for Vocational and Special Training. These are largely used to pay for the social security costs of the teaching staff in these centres.

In addition, there are other European subsidies and grants available, and taking part in competitions and contests also brings economic rewards. The Valencia International Band Contest, which has been held since 1886, is a good example. Although the name, categories and its functioning have changed over time, in 2019 it was celebrated for the 133rd time. Over the years, thousands of bands from around the world have participated in the event (Valencia International Band Contest, 2020). Other musical competitions attended by Valencian bands to obtain financial and prestigious prizes include the Alicante (1971), Valencia (1976) and Castellon (1977)

Image 3 Valencia International Band Contest, 2005 (*Source* Ateneu Musical de Cullera [2020])

provincial band competitions, the Cullera National Band Contest (1947), the Villa de Altea International Band Contest (1949) in Spain and the World Music Contest in Kerkrade (1951) in the Netherlands (Image 3).

1.3 Musical Societies Declared as Cultural Heritage

In 1998, the Valencian Music Law was created to protect musical societies. This law includes measures to promote music and its learning at all levels, so as to promote its dissemination, by creating the means and conditions for the cultural and musical development of civil society. The importance of these bands is reflected in the fact that the Valencia Provincial Council has a deputy delegate in charge of bands, being the only Spanish territory to have this position.

The Valencian Region's musical societies were declared as an Asset of Intangible Cultural Interest in 2018, in Valencian Government Decree 68/2018 of 25th May by the Regional Ministry of Education, Research, Culture and Sports (Generalitat Valenciana, 2018). This declaration is linked to the popular Valencian musical tradition, materialised by the musical societies, as transmitters of intangible heritage.

On 30 March 2021, the Spanish Government declared musical societies in the Valencian Region as a Representative Manifestation of Intangible Cultural Heritage in Spain, taking into account their cultural, educational and social relevance. This declaration protects musical societies, as it safeguards their heritage and ensures their permanence over time, given that this protection is associated with greater financial aid, which will help to alleviate the negative impact caused by the pandemic.

1.4 Musical Societies by Areas

Currently, according to FSMCV data, the Valencian Federations has 557 registered musical societies with 200,000 members (FSMCV, 2020). In addition to this data, the bands are divided into a total of 30 geographical areas (Fig. 1).

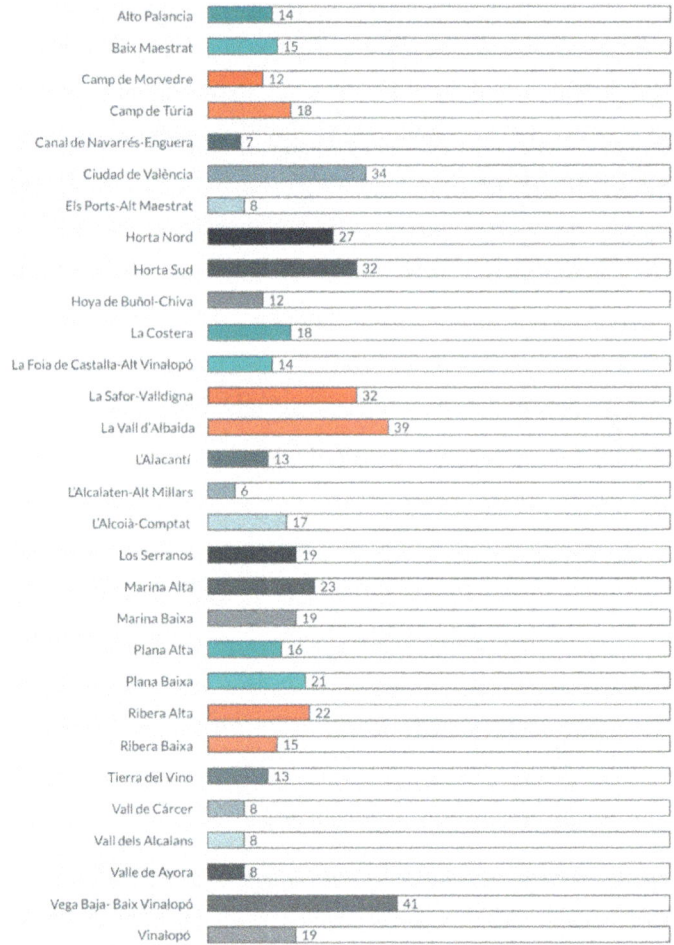

Fig. 1 Musical societies by districts (*Source* Authors' own)

2 The Impact of the COVID-19 Pandemic on Musical Societies

2.1 Current Situation

The pandemic has had a huge impact on the heritage linked to public performances and social relations, given that all the intangible cultural events as well as the musical performances associated with them have all been suspended.

Due to the global pandemic, musical society bands stopped functioning during the state of alarm in Spain, declared on 14 March 2020 by Royal Decree 463/2020 (BOE, 2020) and extended until 21 June 2020, by articles 1 and 2 of Royal Decree 555/2020 on 5 June (BOE, 2020).

During this time, teaching activities moved to an online format overnight in response to safety measures which initially prevented citizens from leaving their homes, and later on required adaptation to new safety regulations to prevent the spread of COVID-19. The musical societies responded to both circumstances by trying to continue the group rehearsals for their bands, choirs, orchestras, music schools and other groups.

2.2 Ethnographic Study of the Impact of the COVID-19

A survey was carried out among registered musical societies in the Valencian Region to assess the extent to which they were affected by the pandemic from March 2020 onwards. The survey was answered by more than 50% of the musical societies. At first, activities were restricted due to the initial lockdown period between March and June 2020, though extensive restrictions remained in place after the first state of alarm. Given this situation, and in their effort to maintain their economic and social activities, these societies had to implement complex prevention measures to ensure safety during rehearsals and had to contemplate the cancellation of acts, events and performances.

The survey was carried out using the Google Forms® tool and centred on the impact the pandemic has had on musical societies' social, economic, artistic and teaching dimensions and on their future. It was sent via email during the month of October 2020 to all musical societies and was also publicised through other social networks.

The surveys were answered anonymously by the musical societies in the 30 geographical areas mentioned above. By area (Fig. 2), l´Horta Sud (14.3%) had the highest number of respondents, followed by the Vall d´Albaida (8.5%), l´Horta Nord (7.6%) and Ciutat de València (7.2%).

In terms of the **social dimension**, the survey aimed to assess losses in the societies' social fabric, in terms of members, by compiling the musical actions they carried out during lockdown and their general assessment of the pandemic's social impact.

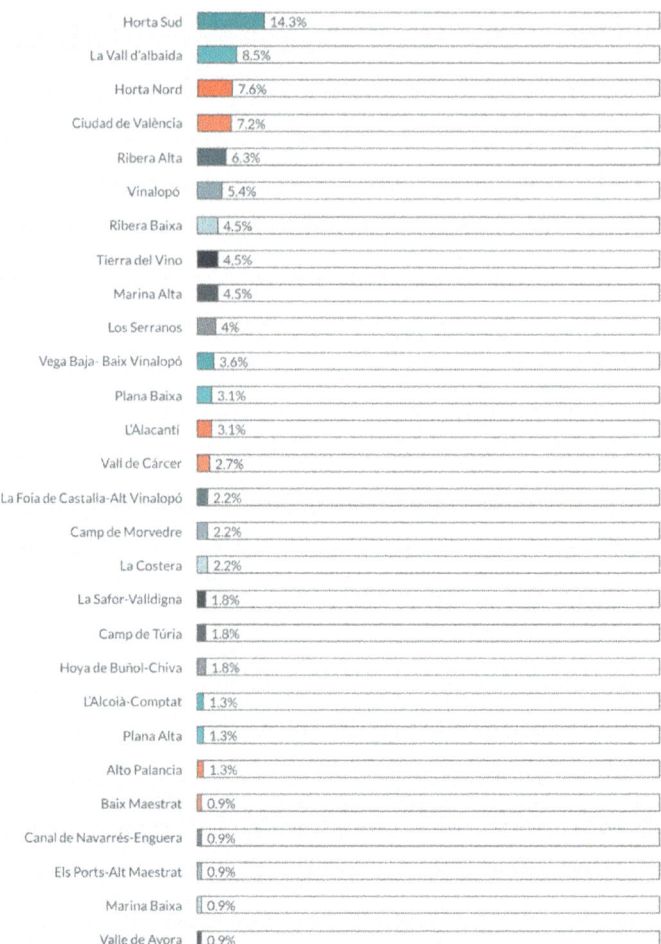

Fig. 2 Survey participation by areas (*Source* Authors' own)

The results obtained in terms of how the social sphere of these musical societies was affected by the pandemic showed responses on a scale of 1–5, in which 1 was the lowest impact and 5 was the highest. The scores were as follows: 2.7% rated the impact suffered as low (score 1); 6.3% rated the impact of the pandemic as moderate (score 2); 20.5% rated a medium impact (score 3); 37.1% rated the impact as high (4 on the scale); and 33.5% considered it as very high, with a 5. Accordingly, 70.6% of musical societies valued the impact of the pandemic in social terms as high or very high (Fig. 3).

Regarding the decline of the social fabric, in terms of number of members after the state of alarm and the suspension of activities, 45.5% declared that they had not lost any members during this period, whilst 54.5% confirmed the opposite. This fact is linked to the financial situation of these musical societies, since fewer members mean

Fig. 3 Impact of the pandemic on musical societies in the social sphere (*Source* Authors' own)

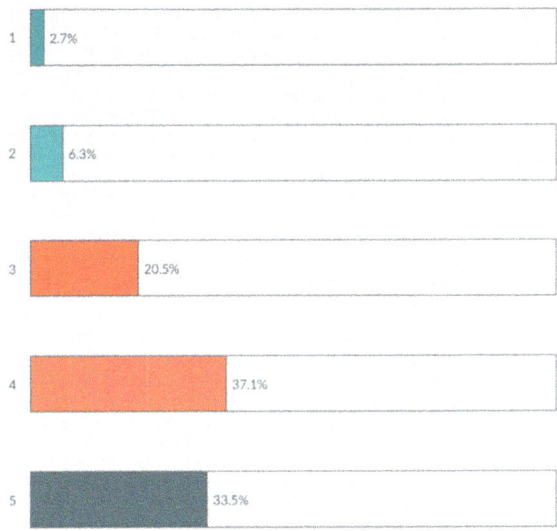

fewer membership fees, producing economic losses that had not been contemplated at the beginning of 2020.

The musical societies performed during lockdown and when the restrictions were alleviated, taking into account health recommendations and legal regulations.

During **lockdown**, performances were given by individual musicians from their homes and were shared through social networks, in an attempt to lift the spirits of the population. In many cases, there were several musicians in the same family and they played together.

89.3% of musical societies declared that individual members had given some kind of individual performance. 84.2% of the groups went out on their balconies to play instruments individually. There were calls through social networks to play the same music which could be heard at the same time, simulating a parade. Parades are a deeply rooted tradition for bands, together with playing musical compositions specifically created for intangible cultural events, like the highly popular, traditional local festivities like the *Fallas* in Valencia, the festivities of *La Magdalena* in Castellon and the *Fogueres de Sant Joan* in Alicante—each of them representing the individual character of their communities.

An example of this took place on 19 March, St. Joseph's Day, which is the day of the patron saint of the city of Valencia. This date is when the *Fallas* figures are burnt in an act known as the *Cremà*. The *Fallas* festival was registered in 2016 on the Representative List of the Intangible Cultural Heritage of Humanity (UNESCO, 2016). On this symbolic day for Valencians, a call to action was put out through social networks to all musicians to play the songs *Paquito el Chocolatero* and *Amparito Roca* in unison, on their balconies and from their windows at midday. This initiative

Image 4 Balcony music in March 2020 (*Source* Agrupación Musical Los Silos de Burjassot [2020])

was organised by FSMCV, which promoted a campaign with the hashtag #FestivalDelsBalcons and the slogan "because we are the land of music, we are going to hit the highest note" (Nuestras Bandas de Música, 2020) (Images 4 and 5).

16.8% of the societies streamed concerts, broadcasting them on social networks and other online platforms. Each musician recorded the concert at home, and then, these recordings were put together. Some of them recorded their local town anthem from their homes, and these were later edited and published. These music-based initiatives managed to strengthen public spirit, which had been severely hit by the pandemic, given the fact that the population had been isolated under lockdown, causing social rupture.

83.2% published videos on social media with individual home recordings, which were later edited and put together. The difficulty of combining tempos and music in this scenario was particularly noteworthy. 59.4% of societies published images on networks. Some of their activities, such as making masks for people in need, which were not directly linked to music broadcasts, had a marked social character.

In the **post-lockdown** period, musical activities continued in other ways, such as parades with the required safety distance between the musicians. For example, the Potríes band marched using specific masks whilst they played (PLÁ, 2020) (Image 6).

These masks were designed, manufactured and marketed by the Sanimusic® brand, which specialises in health and safety for rehearsals and musical events to prevent the risk of contagion caused by COVID-19, under the slogan "we work to keep our culture healthy". The firm sells masks, disinfectant for instruments,

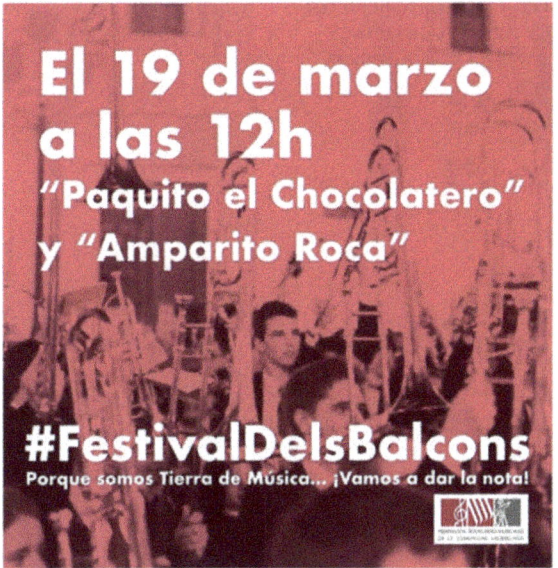

Image 5 Campaign promoted and organised by FSMCV (*Source* Nuestras Bandas de Música [2020])

Image 6 Potries band parading with masks (*Source* Niusdiario [2020])

protection screens and other products. Profits from this venture will go to the Partitura y Territorio foundation (Sanimusic, 2020).

Other activities were carried out outdoors or indoors with limited capacity and with COVID-19 safety measures. Some of them were given financial help from the Valencia Provincial Council, such as the Excellent Band Concerts. Federation-member band exchanges were another of the activities carried out after lockdown. These activities are subsidised by the FSMCV, so the premise was to perform them without inviting another musical society, as though it were a normal concert.

Fig. 4 Economic impact of the pandemic on musical societies (*Source* Authors' own)

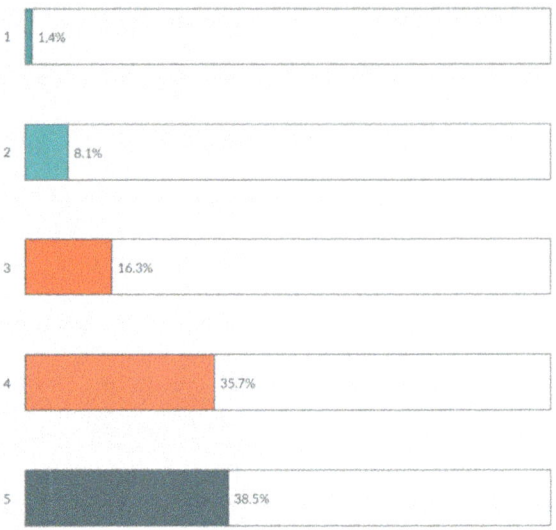

The economic impact of the pandemic on musical societies was also analysed in the survey. The scores ranged from 1 to 5 in which 1 was the lowest economic impact and 5 was the highest. The results were as follows: 1.4% rated the impact as 1; 8.1% rated the impact of the pandemic with a 2; 16.3% rated the impact with a 3; 35.7% rated the impact on their musical society in the pandemic with a 4; and 38.5% rated the impact as very high, with a 5. Therefore, 74.2% of the musical societies estimated the economic impact as being high or very high. These figures are shown below (Fig. 4).

The economic impact was 30.6% due to a decrease in members. 63% of societies lost money as a result of fewer students in their music societies. For 23.7% of these societies, the economic impact was related to payment delays with subsidies. 36.1% had contracts cancelled with town councils and festival associations, and 57.5% had their *Fallas* cancelled as this event could not be held. 60.7% of societies had their Moors and Christians contracts cancelled, whilst 83.1% have been affected by contract cancellations for other festivals. The economic impact has been huge in the sector, given that one of its main sources of income was eliminated, generating losses.

In the **artistic dimension**, we investigated how the bands were affected by the pandemic in their daily activities, i.e. concerts and street performances. The scores ranged from 1 to 5 where 1 responded to the lowest impact and 5 to the highest impact. The results were as follows: 0.5% rated the impact with a score of 1; 2.7% rated the impact of the pandemic with a 2; 12.6% indicated a score of 3; 29.3% of the musical societies rated the artistic impact in the pandemic with a 4; and 55% rated the impact with a 5. In short, 84.3% of musical societies valued the artistic impact as high or very high. These figures are shown below (Fig. 5).

Fig. 5 Artistic impact of the pandemic on musical societies (*Source* Authors' own)

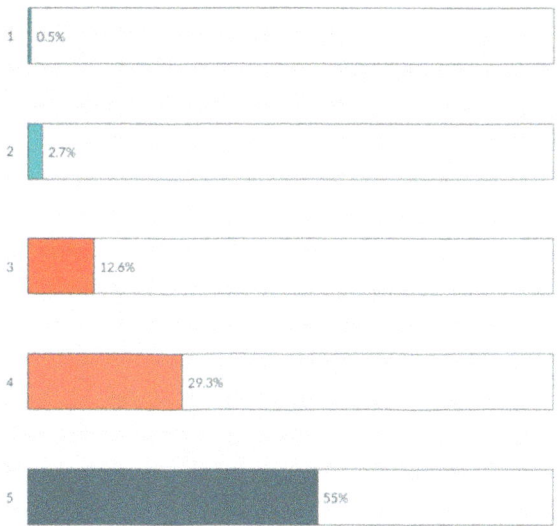

The survey was distributed in October 2020, and a question related to the current situation (at that time) of the bands was included in order to obtain a numerical result of how many of them had resumed rehearsals and performances. 90.6% had been able to resume rehearsals, with the relevant safety measures, and 58.8% had resumed their music performances, complying with the legal measures in force. 41.2% of the bands had not been able to resume their performances and were awaiting improvements in the pandemic figures (Image 7).

70.5% of the musical groups lost band musicians. The losses of musicians were evaluated between 1 and 5, where 1 corresponded to "no musician" and 5 to "a high percentage" of musicians. The results were as follows: 31.2% rated the decrease in musicians with a 1; 28.8% with a 2; 26.5% with a 3; 10.7% rated the decrease with a 4; and 52.8% rated it as very high, with a score of 5. These figures may correspond to temporary losses given the health situation.

The ages of the musicians who left the bands varied. Losses stood at 36.4% of the 12–18 age group; 36.4% of the 19–25 age group; 25.9% of the 26–35 age group; 22.8% of the 36–45 age group. In the 46–55 and 56–65 age brackets, the figures were the same, with the musical societies losing 35.2% in both cases. Finally, 34% of the musicians over 65 years of age have left the bands.

The **teaching dimension** centres on the music schools associated with the musical societies. The survey asked the extent to which these educational institutions had been affected by the pandemic. The respondents were given a scale of 1–5 where 1 was the lowest impact and 5 was the highest. The results were as follows: 11.9% valued the decrease in students with a score of 1; 17% with a score of 2; 25.7% with a score of 3; 33.9% rated the impact on their music school in the pandemic as high, with a score of 4; and 11.5% considered the impact as being very high, with a score of 5.

Image 7 Concert during the post-lockdown period (*Source* Societat Musical "L'Artesana" de Catarroja [2020])

In 92.6% of cases, classes were moved online and were streamed. They were divided into types of complexity by group subjects, such as music theory, band and choir. In these cases, an attempt was made to provide students with online classes, despite the difficulties, peculiarities and needs that each student had, and the problems caused by connection issues and different broadband speeds. These problems could not be solved by 7.4% of music schools, which had to cancel their lessons completely. Less than 8% of these music schools stated that they were waiting for the restrictions to be lifted before resuming classes (Image 8).

During this process of change, there were several working areas in which adjustments had to be made in the teaching staff's situation. 80.6% stated that their employment status with their music schools did not change. However, classes had to be given online, which implied an extra effort and more working hours in order to change the teaching model almost overnight. Most of the schools chose this approach and it worked satisfactorily.

Other activities that took place were the music school auditions which were conducted through social networks. Some societies also carried out other types of projects related to boosting their identity, such as drawing competitions for music school students in order to support a collective sentiment among their members.

However, despite the efforts made by the teaching staff, in some cases, the musical societies stated that they had to reduce fees because the students could not use their

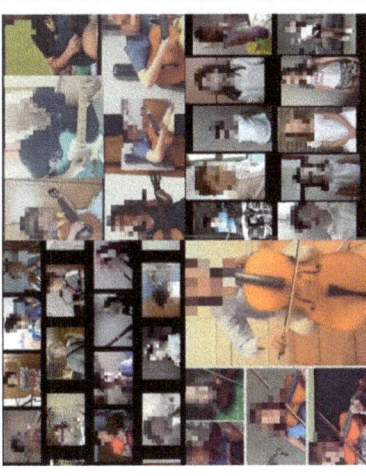

Image 8 Online music classes (*Source* Centre Artístic Musical de Moncada [2020])

facilities, thereby reducing their sources of income. In some cases, schools had to reduce the contract hours of their teachers. Other problems included "online fatigue" of the student body as a result of so many virtual classes, due to the fact that during lockdown, primary schools also gave their classes online. Students got tired of "living online", which led to the early closure of the musical academic year.

Another situation that music schools came up against was the loss of subsidies, which meant they had to resort to applying for bank loans to maintain the teachers' payrolls. In the survey, 19.4% of societies stated that they had had to avail themselves of state aid for furloughing. Some musical societies had to terminate their teachers' contracts, especially for "musical language" and "instrumental ensemble" classes or had to make use of the Spanish Government aid system for symphonic band directors.

Regarding the loss of students in music schools, 11.1% did not suffer losses due to the exceptional situation; 38.5% lost between 1 and 10 students; 20.7% lost between 11 and 20 students; 14.9% suffered losses of between 21 and 30 students; 6.7% lost between 31 and 40 students; 2.9% lost between 41 and 50 students; 2.4% lost between 51-60 students; 0.5% between 61 and 70 students; 0.5% suffered decreases of between 71 and 80 students; and 1.9% stated that they had lost more than 100 students. This situation will cause in the future, a decrease of musicians in musical societies.

The ages at which the drop-out rate was higher were the 5–6 age group, with 23.36%, followed by the 7–8 age group and the 3–4 age group, both with a figure of 19.96%. A 15.19% drop was registered in students between 9 and 10 years of age and the figure was 14.96% in the 11- to 12-year-old groups. In the age of early stimulation, between 0 and 2 years, a decrease of 6.7% in the number of children was registered. This figure is low because few musical societies offer classes for this age group.

In terms of the **future**, 79.4% of them stated that they are now prepared for new closures in their schools, because they have developed alternative systems that have worked well, both for students and for teachers.

86.3% of musical societies explored ways to continue their artistic activities on the Internet and considered that they were ready for possible new suspensions of rehearsals and concerts.

3 Conclusions

Musical societies in the Valencian Region have the ability to boost the collective spirit. They supported society in the pandemic, during lockdown and in the period of isolation, using music as a symbol of social cohesion.

However, the economic impact has been significant in the sector, since one of the main economic sources of income for the bands comes from the contracts they have to play at annual folklore festivals. These affect musicians, because they are paid activities, and also the societies, which receive a percentage of the income.

The pandemic has also had a negative impact on the musical societies' music schools, which made huge efforts to adapt their teaching techniques to a virtual teaching environment, with all the difficulties that this entailed. Significant economic investment was also made to cater for these new needs and new way of teaching.

Throughout the pandemic, musical societies have demonstrated their power of resilience and their adaptability to difficult circumstances and have shown a commendable fighting spirit, defending the cultural, the artistic, the educational and, of course, their social and civic functions.

All of this has been reflected in the altruistic actions carried out to boost public spirits, and in the investments that the majority of musical societies did not hesitate to make in their schools, such as hiring more teachers, health monitoring services and audits to define the distance and capacity of classrooms and auditoriums, dividing class groups and reducing ratios, buying material and reinforcing cleaning and hygiene measures, including machines for purifying the air in classrooms without direct ventilation.

This series of measures should not be forgotten. They continue to be implemented thinking of the students, musicians and the different parts that make up musical societies, which are, after all, a reflection of Valencian society in an intergenerational conglomerate that can bring grandparents and grandchildren together on the same stage, sharing and conveying the same emotions.

Acknowledgements Jesús Escorihuela Castells, President of La Lírica de Silla; Francisco Piñero Sagredo, President of AM Los Silos de Burjassot; Óscar Guillem Martínez, President of SM L'Artesana de Catarroja; Federació de Societats Musicals de la Comunitat Valenciana.

References

Agrupación Musical Los Silos de Burjassot. (2020). Available via AMUSICAL.WIXSITE.COM https://amusical.wixsite.com/lossilos. Accessed 3 June 2020.

Almeria, J. F. (2014). El moviment associatiu de les societats musicals de la Comunitat Valenciana al segle XXI. *Espai Despuig, 8,* 35–44.

Ateneu Musical de Cullera. (2020) Historia. Available via http://www.ateneumusical.com/historia.html. Accessed 7 September 2020.

Ateneu Musical i d´Ensenyament. (2019). *Banda Primitiva de Llíria, 1819–2019. Més de 200 anys de la millor Música.* Ateneu Musical i dÉnsenyament. Available via BANDA PRIMITIVA.ES http://www.bandaprimitiva.es/index.php/es/. Accessed 9 October 2020.

BOE. (2020). *Real Decreto 463/2020, de 14 de marzo, por el que se declara el estado de alarma para la gestión de la situación de crisis sanitaria ocasionada por el COVID-19.* Available via BOE.ES https://www.boe.es/buscar/act.php?id=BOE-A-2020-3692. Accessed 23 October 2020.

Centre Artístic Musical de Moncada. (2020). Available via MUSICALMONCADA.ES https://musicalmoncada.es. Accessed 20 June 2020.

Centro Instructivo Musical Banda de Torrefiel. (2020). *Banda de Torrefiel.* Available via BANDA-TORREFIEL.ES https://bandatorrefiel.es Accessed 19 October 2020.

III Congrés General de Societats Musicals de la Comunitat Valenciana. (2013). *Resum executiu* (Pau Rausell, coord.). Econcult - Universitat de València. Available via https://www.uv.es/cursegsm/PDF/IIICSMCVRE_Val_.pdf. Accessed 9 October 2020.

Escorihuela, J., Gomis, F. X., González, X., Hernández, P., & Soria, F. (2006). *Les Bandes de música de Silla*. A.M. La Lírica de Silla.

Exm. Ayuntamiento de Titaguas. (2020). Banda La Lira. Available via TITAGUAS.ES. http://www.titaguas.es/content/banda-la-lira. Accessed 17 November 2020.

Fernández Vicedo, F. J. (2010). *El clarinete en España: historia y repertorio hasta el siglo XX* (Tesis Doctoral). http://hdl.handle.net/10481/15084.

Ferri Chulio, A. S. (1983). Sueca, 1881–1980. Ed. Grafival S.L.

FSMCV, Federació de Societatas Musicals de la Comunitat Valenciana. (2020). *El Ministerio de Cultura y Deporte inicia la tramitación para declarar Manifestación Representativa del Patrimonio Cultural Inmaterial en España las Sociedades musicales de la Comunidad de Valenciana*. Available via FSMCV. ORG https://fsmcv.org/es/actualidad/noticias/el-ministeri-de-cultura-i-esport-inicia-la-tramitacio-per-a-declarar-manifestacio-representativa-del-patrimoni-cultural-immaterial-a-espanya-les-societats-musicals-de-la-comunitat-de-valenciana. Accessed 20 November 2020.

Generalitat Valenciana. (2018). *Conselleria de Educación, Investigación, Cultura y Deporte. DECRETO 68/2018, de 25 de mayo, del Consell, por el que se declara bien de interés cultural inmaterial la tradición musical popular valenciana materializada por las socieda- des musicales de la Comunitat Valenciana*. Available via DOCV.GVA.ES. http://www.dogv.gva.es/datos/2018/06/01/pdf/2018_5421.pdf. Accessed 9 October 2020

Infopalancia. (2016). Aniversario de la Unión Musical de Caudiel. Available via INFOPALANCIA.COM. https://www.infopalancia.com/aniversario-de-la-union-musical-de-caudiel/. Accessed 9 October 2020.

Las Provincias. (2020). *Las bandas de música de la Comunitat declaradas por el Gobierno como manifestación representativa del patrimonio cultural inmaterial*. Available via LAS PROVINCIAS.ES https://www.lasprovincias.es/culturas/musica/bandas-musica-comunitat-20200727163842-nt.html. Accessed 20 June 2020.

Nuestras Bandas de Música. (2020). *Los músicos valencianos se preparan para dar el Do de pecho*. Available via NUESTRASBANDASDEMUSICA.COM https://www.nuestrasbandasdemusica.com/noticias-nbm/organismos-instituciones/13724-los-musicos-valencianos-se-preparan-para-dar-el-do-de-pecho.html. Accessed 3 November 2020.

PLÁ, C. (2020). *Mascarillas para los músicos y para los instrumentos en el primer pasacalle de una banda de música*. Available via NIUSDIARIO.ES https://www.niusdiario.es/cultura/espectaculos/mascarillas-musicos-instrumentos-primer-pasacalles-banda-musica-potries-valencia_18_2967570176.html. Accessed 20 November 2020.

Ruiz de Lihory, J. (1903). *La música en Valencia. Diccionario biográfico y crítico*. Establecimiento Tipográfico Doménech.

Sanimusic. (2020). *Seguridad en la Música*. Available via SANIMUSIC.NET https://sanimusic.net. Accessed 20 November 2020.

Societat Musical "L´Artesana" de Catarroja. (2020). Available via LARTESANA.ORG http://www.lartesana.org/societat/?lang=es. Accessed 20 June 2020.

UNESCO. (2016). *Valencia Fallas festivity*. Available via UNESCO.ORG. https://ich.unesco.org/en/RL/valencia-fallas-festivity-00859?RL=00859. Accessed 20 June 2020.

Unió Músical D'Albaida "L'Aranya". (2020). *Historia*. Available via http://www.umaaranya.com. Accessed 29 September 2020.

UNIÓN MUSICAL DE MURO (2020). *Música de Banda a Muro 1801–2001*. Available via UNIOMUSICALMURO.ORG https://uniomusicalmuro.org. Accessed 3 June 2020

Unión Musical "Sueños de Artista". (2020). U.M. "Sueños de Artista" de Almedíjar. Available vía TWITTER https://twitter.com/umsuenosartista. Accessed 3 June 2020

Valencia International Band Contest. (2020). Valencia City Council. Available via http://www.cibm-valencia.com/eng/I_historia.aspx. Accessed 20 October 2020.

Vell, F. O. (2014). Las bandas militares en la España de la Restauración (1874–1931). *Nassarre, 30,* 163–194.

Open Access This chapter is licensed under the terms of the Creative Commons Attribution 4.0 International License (http://creativecommons.org/licenses/by/4.0/), which permits use, sharing, adaptation, distribution and reproduction in any medium or format, as long as you give appropriate credit to the original author(s) and the source, provide a link to the Creative Commons license and indicate if changes were made.

The images or other third party material in this chapter are included in the chapter's Creative Commons license, unless indicated otherwise in a credit line to the material. If material is not included in the chapter's Creative Commons license and your intended use is not permitted by statutory regulation or exceeds the permitted use, you will need to obtain permission directly from the copyright holder.

Conclusions: Music as an Economic, Social, Cultural, Creative and Resilient Activity

María de-Miguel-Molina and Virginia Santamarina-Campos

1 Music as a Cultural and Creative Industry in the Literature

The topics covered in this book have been given attention by the literature in the last four years, with studies about CCIs and music increasing over this period, especially in the United Kingdom. However, there is a lack of analysis in their territorial dimension, i.e. how local development (in its economic, political, social and cultural dimensions) is affected by music, such as the case of concert bands in Spain.

In our literature research conducted in Scopus, following the sequence: TITLE-ABS-KEY (music AND cultural AND creative) and limited to the years 2018–2021, we obtained 279 results, from which we selected the most relevant keywords using VosViewer (Van Eck & Waltman, 2020) in order to find some research gaps.

As shown in Fig. 1, different keywords connect music and CCIs as we have done in this book, with the colour of an item being determined by the cluster to which the item belongs (Van Eck & Waltman, 2020). There are studies about the economy of the music industry as CCIs (light blue, chapter 2), the policies that encourage music as CCIs (yellow, chapter 3), the advantages of music as therapy (green, chapter 4), the connection of music as popular culture for young people (red, chapter 5), the role of music as a CCI in local identity (purple, chapter 6) and the importance of creativity in popular music (navy blue, chapter 7).

Therefore, we have added the importance of resilience for CCIs, and especially for musical societies as cultural and creative services. Tschmuck (2003) explained creativity as a collective and disruptive process, and this has been shown through the evolution of the phonographic industry in different cultural paradigms centring on

---

M. de-Miguel-Molina (✉) · V. Santamarina-Campos
Universitat Politècnica de València, Valencia, Spain
e-mail: mademi@omp.upv.es

© The Author(s) 2021
B. de-Miguel-Molina et al. (eds.), *Music as Intangible Cultural Heritage*, SpringerBriefs in Economics,
https://doi.org/10.1007/978-3-030-76882-9_9

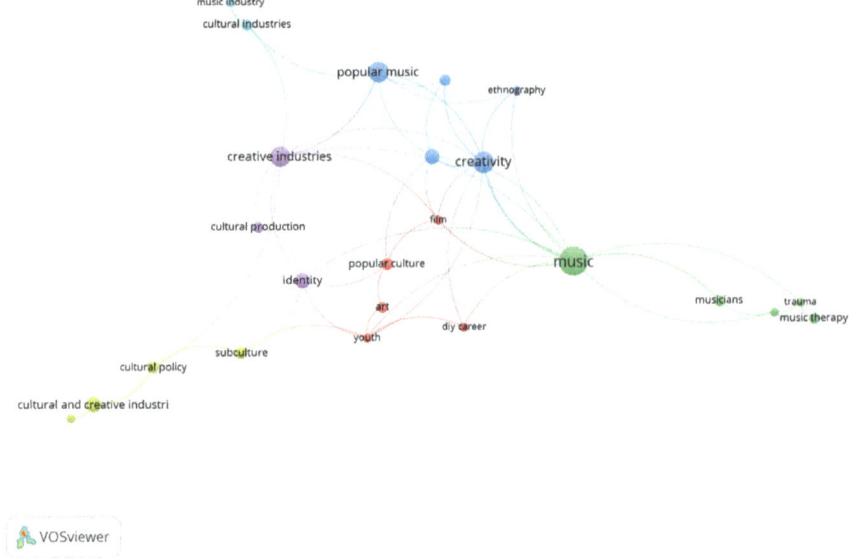

Fig. 1 Co-occurrences of keywords for music and CCIs (*Source* Authors' own with VosViewer [Van Eck & Waltman, 2020])

three main events: the radio (20s), rock and roll (50s) and the Internet (present). The latter has enabled music CCIs to adapt to the global pandemic.

2 Music as a Creative and Economic Activity

The impact of CCIs on the European economy is well known (De Miguel Molina et al., 2012). The music industry is based on four creative chains: creation, reproduction, distribution and consumption. Internet has enabled two phenomena: on the one hand, music consumption structures have experienced a transition to digital formats (web-based digital shops and mobiles). On the other, Internet labels, i.e. platforms for online distribution and promotion in which a piece of music is released for free under a Creative Commons or similar licence (Dellyana et al., 2017), facilitate the fight against piracy. This implies that music, which started as a service and transitioned to a product, has now returned to occupy its space as a service thanks to the Internet but also to the promotion of live concerts and local music heritage.

Within CCIs, the popularity of music has increased despite the current crisis. In "The impact of the music industry in Europe and the business models involved in its value chain", Blanca de Miguel, Rafael Boix and Pau Rausell present an overview of the importance of this sector in Europe (European Commission, 2020) and show how its business models have evolved. The music sector is made up of different activities and companies involved in its value chain, such as production, publishing/reproduction, distribution and exhibition/consumption. All these companies have been influenced by digitalisation, which forces them to increase their rivalry by offering complementary products. The recording industry is still the activity that generates the biggest impact and it is concentrated in just a few big companies, the record labels, for which the streaming services are an important customer segment. In the case of exhibition activities, they have been able to innovate while preserving their mission and cultural heritage, incorporating streaming services. However, a lack of data makes it difficult to evaluate the total impact of all music activities, which explains why few studies have measured its total incidence.

From the point of view of public policies, this sector is worth promoting. In "The role of public policies in enhancing cultural and creative industries: an analysis of public policies related to music in Colombia", Marleny Gómez, Daniel Catalá and María de Miguel have highlighted the importance of music in Bogota given its contribution at a cultural, social and economic level to CCIs in Colombia. In fact, the UNESCO included Bogota in its network of "creative cities of music" in 2012. These advances have been achieved thanks to the creation, development and implementation of public policies that facilitate the musical growth of the country's capital city, together with other CCIs (Alcaldía de Bogotá, 2019). Moreover, public policies linked to CCIs have contributed to reduce social exclusion (Gutiérrez & Sáez, 2018).

In terms of specific innovations, in the chapter "Soundcool: a business model for cultural industries born out of a research project", Nuria Lloret, Jorge Sastre, Crismary Ospina and Stefano Scarani have described the creation process of the Soundcool app, explaining its advantages in different markets and economic sectors: education, music performance, artistic performance, dance and even, in the health sector, contributing to the therapy of people with special needs (Sastre et al., 2020) and helping patients with neurodegenerative diseases. Soundcool started as a non-profit project and it could be classified as a DIY (do-it-yourself) service, but now it needs to incorporate a business model to be able to offer more and better content on the platform in the long term. It has recently an incubator programme which should help the system to move to the next level in the mid-term, through market and financial analysis of the educational field, which is the most developed part of the app (Scarani et al., 2020).

3 Music as a Social and Cultural Activity

Literature has shown important differences in relation to music preferences, social identity, cultural capital and consumption patterns. For example, music consumption has dealt with the issues of alternative music genres and how different genders participate in them. Social networks and music platforms have also played an important role in greater production, accessibility, visibility and knowledge, but also in broader music audiences (Simoes & Campos, 2017). In the chapter "Breaking the gender gap in rap/hip-hop consumption," María-Luisa Palma, Manuel Cuadrado and

Juan-D. Montoro have presented the results of an exploratory survey that enabled them to analyse rap music consumption habits and appreciation of the genre, as well as to segment participants based on satisfaction, interest and knowledge regarding rap/hip-hop. One of the findings revealed the increasing participation of women in rap and their knowledge of the genre. However, when they go to a concert, women usually go with their partners. These findings corroborate previous studies, such as the works by Laidlaw (2011) and Langmeyer et al. (2012).

Moreover, music is the foundation on which many social and cultural groups are created, such as musical societies, which play a cohesive and identity-building role in the communities. This is presented in the case of bands in the Valencian Region (Spain). In "The intangible cultural landscape of the Banda Primitiva de Lliria", Virginia Santamarina, José-Luis Gasent, Pau Alcocer and María Ángeles Carabal analyse how this musical society contributes to positioning creativity and CCIs at the centre of local development, reinforcing identity elements in Lliria and the Valencian Region. This civil band which is the oldest in Spain is presented as an open heritage resource that has developed according to the uses, values and symbols assigned to it by local society. The band has played a key role in boosting the recognition of this form of intangible cultural heritage in social cohesion and development through collective creativity and shared culture, especially in an uncertain situation for CCIs in the pandemic.

Furthermore, in the chapter "Music for the Moors and Christians festivities as intangible cultural heritage: a specific genre for wind bands in certain Spanish regions", Daniel Catalá and Gabino Ponce have specifically analysed the cultural, artistic and economic value of the music composed for and played at the Moors and Christians festivals in the Valencian Region. This music is recognised as one of the most genuine manifestations of Valencian music (UNDEF-FSMCV, 2011). They highlight that a large part of the economic flows that are generated in the local environments of the Moors and Christians festivals is linked to the hiring of bands for musical accompaniment in parades and for the celebration of other activities, such as concerts, recreational performances and recordings. These activities make up a fundamental part of the income sources for many musical societies (Rausell, 2018).

4 Music and Crisis Management

Finally, although music has also been affected by the pandemic, it has yet again shown its resilience in adapting to its consumers. The Valencian Region's musical societies have been able to transmit their collective spirit (Almeria, 2014), supporting society during the lockdown period and using music as a symbol of social cohesion. This is reflected in the chapter "The impact of the COVID-19 pandemic on musical societies in the Valencian Region, Spain", where Angela Carabal, Guillem Escorihuela, Virginia Santamarina and Javier Pérez present the economic impact of the pandemic on these cultural institutions, given that one of their main sources of income is contracts to perform at folklore festivals. This negative impact has also extended to their music schools, which have been forced to adapt to virtual teaching and to make the necessary investments to ensure safety through health monitoring services and audits. The chapter shows how musical societies are a reflection of Valencian society (Generalitat Valenciana, 2018) in an intergenerational group that brings together young and old people in the same space, sharing and conveying the same emotions.

5 Overall Conclusions

This book is a collective effort that has put together different aspects of music to highlight its contribution to CCIs, highlighting how these dimensions (economic, cultural and political) are related and, at the same time, pointing out how they are essential in monitoring the music industry which, in turn, can improve local development. Moreover, the territorial dimension of music as a CCI is necessary to understand the role that music plays in society, in the shape of local festivities, and approaching new generations, for example, through DIY instruments and technological platforms (Chilton, 2020).

In the specific case of civil bands, they have been presented as a local intangible resource that possesses all the dimensions of CCIs: generating economic activity, acting as a force for cohesion in the community and enhancing identity.

The resilience of the music sector has also been highlighted, showing different examples of how music activities have adapted to the challenges posed by the pandemic. In this case, the fact that the sector had already undergone digital transformation has been crucial to ensure its sustainability, although in-person performances are still necessary to continue building social identity and understanding creativity as a collective process, in which people interact with individual artists and groups, such as bands, given that they are key partners for the industry.

References

Alcaldía de Bogotá. (2019). *Guía Práctica para la Creación de Áreas de Desarrollo Naranja*. In Política Pública Distrital de Economía Cultural y Creativa (Secretaria). Bogotá.
Almeria, J. F. (2014). El moviment associatiu de les societats musicals de la Comunitat Valenciana al segle XXI. *Espai Despuig, 8,* 35–44.
Chilton, M. (2020). DIY music: How musicians did it for themselves. *Udiscovermusic*. Available at https://www.udiscovermusic.com/in-depth-features/history-diy-music/. Accessed 25 January 2021.
De Miguel Molina, B., Hervás Oliver, J. L., & De Miguel Molina, M. (2012). The importance of creative industry agglomerations in explaining the wealth of European Regions. *European Planning Studies, 8*(2), 1263–1280. https://doi.org/10.1080/09654313.2012.680579.
Dellyana, D., Simatupang, T. M., & Dhewanto, W. (2017). Business model types associated with network structure changes in the music industry. *International Journal of Business Innovation and Research, 13*(1), 112–129.

European Commission. (2020). *Creative Europe. Monitoring Report 2019*. Publications Office of the European Union, Luxembourg.

Generalitat Valenciana (2018). Conselleria de Educación, Investigación, Cultura y Deporte. *Decreto 68/2018, de 25 de mayo, del Consell, por el que se declara bien de interés cultural inmaterial la tradición musical popular valenciana materializada por las sociedades musicales de la Comunitat Valenciana*. Available via DOCV.GVA.ES http://www.dogv.gva.es/datos/2018/06/01/pdf/2018_5 421.pdf. Accessed 9 October 2020.

Gutiérrez, C. A. B., & Sáez, F. A. A. (2018). Emergencia y configuración del Bronx en Bogotá. The production of urban marginality. The sociohistorical process, emergency and configuration of the Bronx in Bogotá. *Imagonautas, 107*–128.

Laidlaw, A. (2011). *Blackness in the absence of blackness: White appropriations of rap music and hip-hop culture in Newcastle upon Tyne—Explaining a cultural shift* (Thesis). Loughborough University, UK. https://hdl.handle.net/2134/8389.

Langmeyer, A., Guglhör-Rudan, A., & Tarnai, C. (2012). What do music preferences reveal about personality? *Journal of Individual Differences, 33*(2), 119–130. https://doi.org/10.1027/1614-0001/a000082.

Rausell, P. (2018). *Estructura, dimensión e impacto económico de las sociedades musicales*. Universitat de València-FSMCV-Econcult.

Sastre, J., Lloret, N., Scarani, S., Dannenberg, B., & Jara, J. (2020). Collaborative creation with soundcool for socially distanced. *Conference KEAMSAC2020*, Seoul, Korea.

Scarani, S., Muñoz, A., Serquera, J., Sastre, J., & Dannenberg, R. (2020). Software for interactive and collaborative creation in the classroom and beyond: An overview of the soundcool software. *Computer Music Journal, 43*(4), 12–24.

Simoes, J. A., & Campos, R. (2017). Digital media, subcultural activity and youth participation: The cases of protest rap and graffiti in Portugal. *Journal of Youth Studies, 20*(1), 16–31. https://doi.org/10.1080/13676261.2016.1166190.

Tschmuck, P. (2003). How creative are the creative industries? A case of the music industry. *The Journal of Arts Management, Law, and Society, 33*(2), 127–141.

UNDEF-FSMCV. (2011). *Convenio UNDEF-FSMCV para el establecimiento de unos acuerdos de mínimos que regularán las relaciones entre ambas entidades y sus asociados*. UNDEF-FSMCV.

Van Eck, N. J., & Waltman, L. (2020). *VOSviewer Manual* (version 1.6.14). University of Leiden.

Open Access This chapter is licensed under the terms of the Creative Commons Attribution 4.0 International License (http://creativecommons.org/licenses/by/4.0/), which permits use, sharing, adaptation, distribution and reproduction in any medium or format, as long as you give appropriate credit to the original author(s) and the source, provide a link to the Creative Commons license and indicate if changes were made.

The images or other third party material in this chapter are included in the chapter's Creative Commons license, unless indicated otherwise in a credit line to the material. If material is not included in the chapter's Creative Commons license and your intended use is not permitted by statutory regulation or exceeds the permitted use, you will need to obtain permission directly from the copyright holder.

GPSR Compliance

The European Union's (EU) General Product Safety Regulation (GPSR) is a set of rules that requires consumer products to be safe and our obligations to ensure this.

If you have any concerns about our products, you can contact us on

ProductSafety@springernature.com

In case Publisher is established outside the EU, the EU authorized representative is:

Springer Nature Customer Service Center GmbH
Europaplatz 3
69115 Heidelberg, Germany

www.ingramcontent.com/pod-product-compliance
Ingram Content Group UK Ltd.
Pitfield, Milton Keynes, MK11 3LW, UK
UKHW021953040925
462611UK00004B/421